D0268889

How Far Is the
Nearest Pint?

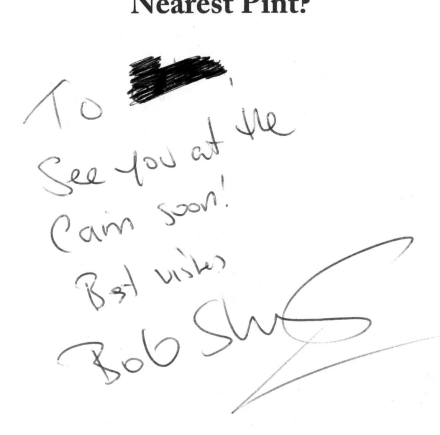

To ~~████~~

See you at the

Cam soon!

Best wishes

Bob Shw

How Far Is the Nearest Pint?

Bob Shields

Black & White Publishing

First published 2006
by Black & White Publishing Ltd
99 Giles Street, Edinburgh EH6 6BZ
in association with
Goatbrain Publishing
A division of Goatbrain Ltd
7 Barnes Terrace
Ayr KA7 2DB

ISBN 13: 978 1 84502 139 9
ISBN 10: 1 84502 139 8

Copyright © Bob Shields 2006

The right of Bob Shields to be identified as the author of this work has been asserted by him in accordance with the Copyright, Designs and Patents Act 1988.

All rights reserved. No part of this publication may be reproduced, stored in a retrieval system, or transmitted in any form, or by any means, electronic, mechanical, photocopying, recording or otherwise, without permission in writing from the publisher.

Cover photography: Martin McCready @ Upfront Photography.

Cover design: Frontpage

A CIP catalogue record for this book is available from the British Library.

Printed and bound by Bell & Bain Ltd

For the Original Bob, Laura and Lisa.
Special thanks to the foot soldiers of the *Ayrshire Post*,
Evening Times, *Daily Record* and *Sunday Mail*
who helped me along the way.
Thanks also to Anna, Billy, Del, Charlie, Ronnie, Tales
and others for the Copy Cat years.
To Maurice and Hazel, Don and Spud in Aviemore
To Roberto, Owen and Kirstin and the Ayr mob
To Nigel and everyone at the Old Bridge Inn
To Caroline and everyone at the Cairngorm Hotel
To Paul and everyone at the Bon Accord
To Elaine and everyone at the Ben Nevis
… and to publicans worldwide!

In fond memory of …

'The Wee Mammy'
'JB'
'Big Pete'
'Paddy'

Contents

Three-star Michelin chef Gordon teaches five-star diddy Bob how to make a simple omelette

Foreword

So the big man has finally finished his book. About time! F**k me! He's been telling me about it for long enough.

When I finally got my copy, I opened it up and there he is grinning at me with the usual Guinness in front of him. I had to laugh – I've known him for almost ten years and never seen him without it.

And I was pleased to read I was partly responsible for Bob running the New York Marathon. What was your time, Bob? Five hours? For f**k's sake, I've made sauces that run faster than that.

Anyway, the whole point of a foreword is to say nice things about the author. So what can I say about Bob Shields? Well, he usually turns up at my door with a present for the kids. And he bought me a Rangers tie once. He makes an almost edible omelette. And … er … that's about it really.

But Bob's been a journalist all his life – and his background reminds me a little of my own. I spent most of my adult life in kitchens, working nights and weekends and quietly learning and gaining experience – long before a TV camera ever appeared.

Bob's story is much the same, putting in years of hard work and learning his craft, before becoming the top writer with the country's top paper.

You get out of life what you put into it.

And if you can have a laugh along the way – and this book is full of them – then I say f*****g good luck to you.

Gordon Ramsay
London 2006

To Fiona – HITYL

1

Where Can I Get a Decent F*****g Pint of Guinness Around Here?

WHEN the great and good of the world of celebrity deign to mingle with the great unwashed – that's us journalists! – their agents and press and publicity strategists have a number of formats to chose from.

On top of the heap are personal appearances on television shows like Jonathan Ross or Richard and Judy. At the bottom of the food chain, local newspapers usually have to make do with a press release or maybe a copy of a tame 'question and answer' interview the artists' representatives have prepared themselves.

In between are the national newspapers and magazines, all hell bent on getting something bigger, better – and preferably earlier – than their rivals.

Nothing gets an editor's hormones cranking like the magical word 'exclusive'. I don't think I've ever been to an editorial morning conference and not heard the boss ask at least once, 'Have we got this to ourselves?'

The constant demand for that elusive exclusive has more or less consigned the old fashioned 'press conference' to the world of sport where the pooling of questions and answers is an expedient solution.

Yes, they have their exclusives as well. But they are usually the result of relationships and trusts forged over the years between individual players, managers and journalists.

But when it comes to showbiz, the 'press conference' system just doesn't rock the modern editor's boat.

The moment a rival journalist comes through the door, the world 'exclusive' leaves by the window.

At the same time, movie or record companies are loath to sell their jewels to one single publication, no matter how big. They want maximum exposure – they want to be in every newspaper and magazine.

The solution they came up with was the 'sit down' – also known as the 'one-on-one', 'head-to-head' or 'face-to-face'. And it does exactly what it says on the tin.

The production company involved produce their celebrity and each journalist gets an allotted time for their private chat. Hey presto! They all walk away with their own individual 'exclusive interview'. And if the publication date is agreed in advance – 'embargoed' as we say in the trade – all the 'exclusives' hit all the papers at the same time. And everybody's happy.

Well, to tell the truth, not everybody is happy. In fact, some editors are exceedingly unhappy. Having read what all their rivals managed to extract from an identical situation, they can quickly judge who got the best interview. And if it's not yours … it's not nice!

Sir Alex Ferguson doesn't have exclusive rights to the 'hairdryer' technique and Gordon Ramsay didn't invent 'bollocking' either. Even worse, most of us have enough professional nous to know it's coming!

But even a few stiff ones in the local boozer can't prepare you for the inevitable phone call from the editor's secretary, 'The boss wants to see you.' But to be fair to the editors involved – and I'm working under No. 6 at the *Daily Record* – they would be the first to compliment you if the situation was in the reverse.

Before I leave the subject of 'arse kickings', I feel duty bound to share with you the experience of one reporter who fell foul of his news editor. The whole office knew he was in for some heavy verbals and, sure enough, the news editor arrived and summoned the poor guy to the infamous 'wee room'. What a doing he got. They both emerged, red faced, to a very silent editorial floor.

Some time later, the reporter went to the loo, hastily followed by several colleagues, anxious to hear first hand what had been said.

The reporter, let's call him Stuart, was indignant. 'I just told the bastard to his face. He might be my boss, but I told him I wasn't taking any f*****g shit. I'm telling you boys, it'll be a long time before that w****r tries to play the tough guy with me again ...'

Then a voice emerged from behind a cubicle, it was the calm but unmistakable tone of the news editor. 'Stuart, that's not exactly my recollection of our recent conversation.'

Meanwhile, back at 'face to face' interviews, and back in April 2000, I got a call from a contact offering me a 'sit down' with actor Richard Harris. I was so excited, I went to the pub and even passed my fags round.

The legendary actor had been a hero of mine since his movie *A Man Called Horse*. He was also a bit of a 'hell-raiser' – the polite way we journos imply that he liked a good bucket. Harris was my kind of man.

I was told the seventy-year-old actor wanted to publicise his new film *To Walk With Lions*, a movie based on the final years of George Adamson, the conservationist of *Born Free* fame. But Harris rarely did the press circuit and would never have tied himself to a contract that included mandatory media junketing.

He must have taken some pride in his lion movie – hey, the old puns are the best puns – and volunteered to do the publicity stuff himself. That excited me even more.

It was agreed that I would meet him at London's posh Savoy hotel. Wonderful.

My allotted 'sit down' would be twenty minutes. Not quite so wonderful. The time for the interview would be 5.30pm. Not wonderful at all.

When Harris speaks, the world listens and I knew all the big hitters would be getting their slots as well. I also reckoned 5.30pm would be the fag end of his shift. After a morning and afternoon flow of journalists asking him mostly the same questions, the poor old geezer would be bored out of his tits. But I'd worry about that later. Top of my priority list was to delve into his background and find out as much about Richard Harris as possible.

In journalism, a little research goes exactly that far – a little. If I was going to be his 'fag-end' interview, I'd try and be the best informed fag end he'd ever met. The tiniest snippet of background can sometimes give you an edge.

I once did a telephone interview with the superb Scots actor Ken Stott, star of *The Vice* and other quality television dramas. During my research I discovered his son had a birthday the day before our scheduled chat.

During the initial interview pleasantries, I asked 'Did the wee man have a nice birthday yesterday?' There was a short pause before Ken came back, 'Christ … you've done your homework!' I'll never know if my question did the rest of the interview any good – but I know for certain it didn't do it any harm.

My Richard Harris 'homework' was fascinating stuff. I didn't know he had seven brothers and sisters. I wasn't aware he suffered two years as a bed-ridden teenager, tortured with tuberculosis. Or that he spent a decade learning his craft in rural theatres before *This Sporting Life* made his name and earned him an Oscar nomination in 1963.

I also discovered why The Savoy was the preferred venue for his 'media day'.

Harris had booked a suite there in 1987 ... and never checked out again.

Now that's what I call style! But the Harris 'style' didn't always suit The Savoy. He steadfastly refused to adopt the 'Grill Room' dress code of jacket and tie for dinner. But rather than starve their long standing and most famous resident, the waiters simply put screens around him and hid the scruffy actor from the rest of their diners.

I moved my research on to The Savoy itself. After thirteen years, Harris would know the place and its history inside out, and there might be other anecdotal nuggets about his tenure. There weren't – but it still made for great reading.

Sir Winston Churchill was a regular diner and always sat at table No. 4. When he died, the management kept it vacant for a year as a mark of respect. The Grill Room was so popular within the Palace of Westminster, it was also known as the 'second House of Lords'. One particular peer used to take a short cut and arrived for lunch by scaling a fire escape and climbing through the dining room window.

There was a famous incident when a cocktail waiter spilled a Bloody Mary down actress Sophia Loren's ample cleavage. His excuse to the head waiter was that he'd been distracted by a mouse darting across the dining room floor. Aye, that'll be right! Who looks at the floor when Sophia's flashing her yah-yahs?

The Queen Mother was another regular visitor, but The Savoy could never dare threaten her privacy by putting her name on the reservations list. The head waiter thought she looked like his granny – so she was booked under the name 'grandmother'.

By this time, I probably had enough material for a great feature – and I hadn't even met Richard Harris yet!

On the morning of the interview I flew to London. Sadly, but not unexpectedly, the *Daily Record*'s budget wouldn't quite stretch to booking me into The Savoy. I was quite looking forward to puffing a Churchillian cigar after dinner at table No. 4. So I threw my bag off at my usual London gaff, the Stakis Hilton on Edgware Road, then jumped in a cab.

The journey from the lobby of the Hilton to the lobby of The Savoy is only ten minutes – but it was like going back a hundred years. A doorman in a top hat opened the cab for me then welcomed me into The Savoy's glass and oak panelled splendour. Bell boys in gold trimmed uniforms were buzzing around, their trolleys piled high with wobbling luggage.

I used my mobile to call Ginny, the public relations girl putting it all together. 'I'm in The Savoy lobby,' I told her. 'So am I, I'm sitting at a table by one of the sofas', she replied. I quickly looked around, there were tables every-where, and Fiona Phillips hadn't seen so many sofas. 'It's near the entrance to the American Bar …' she added helpfully. I'd read about the American Bar; apparently it's got some famous black and white photographs on its walls and Noel Coward was prone to tickling its grand piano after a couple of gin and tonics of an evening.

I introduced myself to Ginny, she was tall, dark haired, pretty and immaculately dressed in a business-like suit. In other words, just like every London public relations female I've ever met. If these agencies employ anything other than good lookers, they certainly don't let them out in daylight.

'Richard's running a little late,' she told me, running her finger down a typed list of names. For those of us old enough to have worked in newspapers in the 'hot metal' days, where the slugs of type are a reverse image, reading upside down is not a problem.

I scanned Ginny's list and wasn't too surprised to see *The Times*, the *Daily Mail*, the *Daily Telegraph* and several well-known magazines listed. And yes, right at the bottom, the *Daily Record*.

'I doubt if he'll be ready for you until after six.' We both checked our watches; it was only 5.15pm. 'Can I get you a coffee or something?' she asked.

'No, no thanks, I think I'll go for a stroll,' I said, my eyes fixed firmly on a little arrow with 'American Bar' printed above.

I can't remember much about the famous photographs; I was probably getting over the shock of paying over a fiver for a rum and Coke. And I was getting worried about Mr Harris. What if he decided he wasn't going past his expected 6.00pm finish?

I could picture him up in his room saying, 'Bob who? From the Daily what?

Scotland? Tell him to f**k off! I'm not doing any more!'

I went back to seek the reassurance of the lovely Ginny. 'Maybe another ten minutes,' she smiled.

'He must have had a long day. I hope he's not getting fed up?' I asked.

'Oh, he's fine. But he keeps asking for bottles of water. I think his throat is probably getting a little tired.'

During my research, I'd read that Harris had stopped drinking alcohol well over ten years ago. He famously bowed out of the world of bevvy with two 1957 bottles of claret at £1700 a pop.

'If this is going to be my last drink, I might as well make it a good one,' he was quoted at the time.

'Bottles of water? Changed days ...' I said to Ginny.

'Is he ... er ... still off the alcohol?' I ventured further.

'More or less. He hasn't touched the hard stuff for years, but he does love the odd pint of Guinness.' Ah ... a man after my own heart!

Ginny's mobile buzzed and she spoke a few words before switching off.

'Richard's ready to see you. Just follow me.'

A lift hoisted us heavenwards then Ginny marched off in front down a long, thickly carpeted corridor. From the moment I was given this assignment, I'd wondered what my first captivating question would be to the man who had already been asked everything all day. Now, here I was standing at his door, and I still didn't have a clue.

Ginny knocked politely and the great man opened the door almost immediately.

'Richard, Bob Shields from the *Daily Record* in Scotland ...'

We shook hands and I got my first look at the stage and screen legend. His grey hair was long, almost shoulder length and he had a snow white, neatly trimmed beard. His complexion was the ruddy red of a man who had obviously enjoyed washing down life with a glass or three. But he was tall, broad shouldered and didn't look anything close to his seventy years.

He beckoned me to an armchair while he spoke to Ginny about some phone call he was expecting. The room was small, some kind of ante-room with a sofa, two chairs and some French looking furniture.

This was obviously not the Harris home for the last thirteen years. But I suppose a largely private individual was hardly likely to let the world's press traipse around his front room.

Ginny left and he finally flopped gently on the sofa. 'Well, Bob, what do you want to know? And please call me Richard.'

Armed with the knowledge that here was a no-nonsense, plain-speaking lover of the black throat-charmer, off I went.

'Well Richard, what I really wouldn't mind knowing is … where can I get a decent f*****g pint of Guinness around here? Every time I come to London the Guinness is always crap.'

I wasn't sure if he'd appreciate my rustic use of language. But I was more than certain nobody had asked him that one all day.

Richard – well, I now have his permission to call him that – blinked twice and his eyes widened. A little smile played along his obviously dried out lips.

'My dear fellow, that's very interesting, I know the very place. They import the stuff direct from Dublin rather than the stuff they brew over here.

Do you know The Strand at all?'

Suddenly, he was on his feet, his arms waving and pointing directions to a pub called the Coach and Horses.

'A Scotsman who likes Guinness? I thought you were all whisky drinkers up there. Ah … I used to love a fine malt …'

It was time for a serious bit of name dropping. 'An old pal of yours, Oliver Reed, he got me started on it. We had a two-day session over at his place in Ireland.'

'Where exactly?' he asked. Only later did it occur to me that his question might be a test of whether I was telling the truth – or was Olympic standard bull-shitting. For once, I wasn't.

'Churchtown … O'Brien's I think.'

He threw his head back and laughed. 'Churchtown! Christ, I could tell you some stories. He was a f*****g hell of man. A hell of a man.' He then seemed to catch himself for a second, as if suddenly remembering that his old hell-raising pal was no longer with us.

Then he was animated again. 'Listen, Bob, why don't we do this over a pint?'

God, I need to get out of this room,' he said, gesticulating at the empty bottles of water and a plate of curling sandwiches on the table between us. 'Do you have time? Would you mind?'

Would I mind? Would I mind going for a pint with Richard f*****g Harris? 'I'm always up for a Guinness,' I nodded, trying to contain my excitement.

He pumped his fingers into his mobile and Ginny was at the door within seconds. 'We're going to do this over a pint. Bob is the last one today, isn't he?'

'Yes, but we have some phone calls to make, remember? Ginny had just thrown a giant spanner into my pint with Richard. Suddenly she wasn't so pretty after all.

'Jesus. I forgot about that.'

He ran his hands through his grey hair and thought for a few seconds.

'Right, you give Bob directions to the Coach and Horses. Then we make the calls from my room, then we meet Bob in say … thirty minutes?'

Ginny looked at me and nodded. I looked at Richard and nodded. Richard picked up his glasses and headed for the door. 'Thirty minutes, see you there …' and he was off.

Ginny reached for her mobile; this clearly wasn't part of her plan for the evening. Some lucky boyfriend somewhere was going to have to wait a bit longer for whatever he was waiting for.

'He's never done this before, he doesn't really like journalists,' she muttered. 'What on earth did you say to him?'

'It's … er … a Guinness thing.'

We went back down the lift and through the lobby to the front door. It was now about 6.30pm and the city was in its last throes of rush hour. She gave me my directions – turn right, second left, the pub was opposite a theatre etc. – then she disappeared inside.

My mind was buzzing with all kind of positive thoughts. Going for a pint with Richard Harris had to be better than anything the other journalists had got. What a result! Arse-kickings all round for everyone except Bob!

Wait a minute – they'd want pictures – and I had no time to hire a London freelance photographer. And Richard might not want his picture taken anyway – no photographers was all part of the 'sit down' deal with Ginny's people.

So I dashed across the road to a WHSmith and bought a little disposable camera. It might come in handy.

It was just then that my mind started buzzing again … but this time with negative thoughts. What if he didn't turn up? Maybe he'd change his mind or Ginny would remind him how much he disliked journalists. The bitch! And I didn't even have a single quote in my notebook. Your can't exactly fill a centre spread on Richard Harris giving you directions to a boozer. And all the other journos would have their stories. Oh no. Tomorrow, Bob was going to be arse-kicking central.

I nervously made my way to the pub, it was bustling with city folk having an after work drink and a crowd of guys wearing bow ties. Sherlock Shields quickly deduced they were the musicians from the theatre across the road. But I suppose the trumpets and violin cases were a bit of a giveaway.

I cased the joint for a suitable spot to secrete Mr Harris, and ordered my first pint of the Irish nectar.

'Hello, Bob!' said a voice from behind me. I wheeled round and there stood John Millar, a former *Daily Record* colleague and now a top movie journalist who travelled all over the world meeting the biggest stars.

Remember what I said about another journalist coming through the door and an exclusive going out the window?

Much as though it's nice to see a friendly face in a strange city, I was hoping John would disappear before Richard arrived. No, I wasn't hoping … I was praying like hell. I blustered my way through a bit of conversation, probably watching who was coming through the door more than listening to my friend.

'Another drink, John?'

'No thanks, Bob, I've got an important meeting to keep.' Then he drained his glass and bid me a friendly farewell.

Richard finally arrived, in a tweedy-looking jacket and a hat pulled over his head, along with Ginny. A few people glanced and whispered, obviously recognising him, but I got the feeling his face was a regular feature here. I ordered a pint for Richard, a mineral water for the ever professional Ginny and we got bar stools overlooking a window.

Naturally, we talked about the movie first. *To Walk With Lions* was a dramatic, violent and moving account of George Adamson's gradual decline and eventual murder as his Kenyan lion rehabilitation camp became a target for poachers and bandits.

He told me he felt privileged to have worked beside Ian Bannen in one of his last movies and of how he had it written into his contract that he wouldn't have to work with 'live' animals.

'I wanted them to use body doubles. I hadn't survived all

I'd been through only to end up in a lion's stomach in the middle of bloody nowhere,' he laughed.

But gradually, the mighty beasts worked their magic on the frightened actor.

'I talked to them every morning and they got used to me – or more importantly, my scent.'

More Guinness arrived and Ginny, satisfied I'd got the movie story she's paid to sell me, disappeared. 'You two seem to be doing fine,' she said. We were doing very fine indeed.

Richard pointed to a little Guinness badge, in the shape a filled pint glass, I had pinned to my lapel. 'I do like that,' he smiled.

I made up a story that I wore it everywhere I went.

'It means I'm never too far away from a Guinness,' I joked, 'Fantastic idea, I must get one myself!' he roared.

'Take this one, I've got lots more at home,' I said as I unfastened the little pint.

He was grinning like a little boy as he fixed it onto his own jacket.

'Where I come from, if a man gives you a pint, you give him one back!' he laughed, and headed off to the bar for another round.

We talked about movies, rugby, drink, football, women, movies and drink. But mostly about drink.

He told me how he and Peter O'Toole, Richard Burton and Anthony Hopkins once went on a bender at London's posh Dorchester Hotel. Suitably bevvied, they ordered every bottle on the gantry, including £200 cognacs, and piled into a taxi. They ended up in London's tough East End where they drank the night away on a pavement, handing out drinks to passing down-and-outs.

Another of his favourite tales was of the time his estranged wife's lawyer put a private detective on his tail.

'He followed me everywhere, but I was on to him and even had his mobile number. I used to phone him up from a bar and say, "Hey, I'm pissed out my brains, can you tell me where I am please?"'

My drinking adventures couldn't compete with the master, but I did have a little pub party trick.

'Have you ever seen whisky and water in the same glass but not mixed together?' I asked.

Richard scratched his head. 'Damned impossible I'd say. But I'd never bet against a Scotsman about anything to do with whisky!'

I did my little piece of magic and he peered at the glass through his thick brown spectacles.

'Christ, I wish I'd been shown this years ago. I could have made fortunes …' He was clearly enjoying himself.

I told him about Ginny's comment that journalists are not meant to be his favourite people.

'Well, I don't mind the ones that like Guinness, I suppose,' he countered.

'But I don't normally do the press thing. After *Unforgiven*, they wanted me to do media stuff but I refused.

'They had Clint Eastwood, Gene Hackman and Morgan Freeman, what the f**k did they want an old fart like me for?'

By now, I reckoned he was sufficiently relaxed for me to mention the camera still burning a hole in my pocket. I had quotes and anecdotes to die for – but no picture.

'Can I ask someone to do a picture of us. Holding our pints?'

He nodded and grinned, 'But only if I'm holding a full one!' It was back to the bar for another round. A friendly customer took the picture and a print still hangs in my house – my Guinness badge on Richard's lapel is clearly visible.

We were halfway though our drinks when Richard looked at his watch.

'Christ, it's time to go.'

'Where are you going?' I asked.

'Where are WE going you mean! Follow me!'

He grabbed his hat and dived out the door, by the time I gathered my briefcase and coat, he was halfway back to The Savoy.

'Where are we going?' I asked breathlessly.

'This way, this way,' he urged.

We went up a side street at the Savoy and though a door. Suddenly we were in another pub, though not quite so busy.

'This is the Coal Hole,' Richard explained. 'It used to be where the hotel kept their supply for heating the rooms. Now, it's a little pub. Sorry the Guinness isn't as good as the last place, but I've come here for a reason.'

We were having our first sips when a man arrived through a side door, looking hot and tired.

'Here's my reason now,' he said, and he ordered the man a drink.

'Bob, if you are ever going to stay in a hotel for any length of time, make sure you buy the chef a drink when he's finished.'

We talked food together for a little while and it must have started making Richard feel hungry. Suddenly he put his glass down and declared 'That's me, I'm off. You take care Bob'.

And he disappeared through the same door as the chef arrived.

'Getting Richard to go drinking with anyone is quite a feat, How did you wangle it?' asked the chef.

'Er … it's a Guinness thing,' I told him.

2

The New York Marathon –
Getting to the Starting Line

EDITORS will tell you that the measure of a good journalist is the thickness of his 'contacts book'. This highly prized list of telephone numbers can range from a lollipop-lady in Luss to Rod Stewart's personal assistant in Los Angeles.

These people usually all have one thing in common – you can trust them to tell you the truth. And in return, they trust you not to betray a confidence or write a story that compromises their position with their employer. Top of the range contacts can take years to develop.

If you get really lucky, you eventually miss out the media middlemen and build up a relationship with the person who is central to your story in the first place. I like to think I have an excellent relationship with one of my favourite 'contacts', super chef Gordon Ramsay.

I have met garrulous Gordon more times than ... well, maybe hot dinners isn't the right analogy. I have been to his former flat by the Thames, cooked omlettes in his incredible home in Wandsworth, interviewed him in his old Glasgow restaurant, an Edinburgh boozer and on the roof of serially dodgy hotel in Hollywood, California.

In thirty wonderful years in this game, I have met only two people who I can honestly describe as truly inspirational. The kind of personality you interview and leave muttering, 'F**k me – what a guy!'

One is motor racing legend Jackie Stewart – the other is Gordon Ramsay.

It was in his restaurant in Royal Hospital Road, Chelsea, that Gordon uttered the remark that would leave an indelible mark on my life and lead to one of the proudest – and most painful – moments of my career.

It is hardly a Churchillian or Shakespearian classic but 'Hey, you fat bastard, I bet you couldn't run a f****g marathon,' had all the classic ballsy Ramsay hallmarks.

He had been telling me about his training for the London marathon and suddenly seized on it as a challenge to get me in shape. But I had other ideas.

'Gordon, if I wanted to tour the streets of London, I'll get a f****g taxi, thank you! But make it Sydney, Hong Kong or Rio and I might get excited enough to get my running shoes out!'

'You're on!' he said, with that Hell's Kitchen grin of his. Oh shit … what had I done?

As the Heathrow Express whizzed me back to the airport for my journey home, my mind was already working on a feature idea involving running a marathon. But which one? If I was genuinely going to train and take it seriously, the attraction had to be something better than pounding through the pissing rain in Putney.

Back at the office, I typed 'marathon' into the internet and a hundred screens filled up. Race preparation tips, running shoe adverts, medical advice – trying to kill yourself over twenty-six miles was clearly a popular business.

Eventually I found a timetable of official marathons – and there were hundreds of them. All the major cities were there: London, Paris, Rome, Amsterdam, Hong Kong, Sydney – plus dozens of smaller marathons in places I'd never even heard of. On average, in any given weekend of the year, you have around ten to choose from.

Sadly, I had to rule out some of the more glamorous ones almost immediately. Gordon runs a tight diary and I couldn't see him taking a week out his life just to watch me expire and collapse on the streets of Sydney or Singapore. But I also had to factor in the journalistic side as well. Even with Gordon on board, I couldn't see the editor getting excited about us trotting around Belfast or Plymouth.

For a while, I looked carefully at Athens. After all, this was where it all began and I could imagine Gordon getting a hard-on about running the original Marathon to Athens route that gave the race its name. And in two years' time, this would be the course for the 2004 Olympic marathon.

But Athens also had a downside. The course was a nightmare, especially for a marathon virgin like me. A little graphic on the official race web site appeared to show that the first eight or nine miles were uphill! And the course was only 'open' for five hours, which was pretty much the time I could reasonably expect to finish – if I finished at all.

Running against the distance would be tough enough without running against the clock. If you took over five hours, and didn't get an official time to prove you completed the course, what was the point?

Imagine completing about twenty-five miles, getting in sight of the finishing line, only for a big Greek polis to put his hand up and say 'Sorry pal, that's the Olympic Stadium shut for tonight. But it's open at ten tomorrow.'

Athens was out. I looked at the list again and one city's name suddenly leapt out at me ... New York. Shit! Now why didn't I think of it before?

The Big Apple fitted the bill perfectly. Even before the Twin Towers horror, it was always a dramatic city and one of my favourites. Now, post 9/11, there was more interest in it than ever. It would be an amazing place to write about – and Central Park, the Empire State Building and the concrete canyons of Manhattan are a photographer's dream.

The course looked doable. There were few uphill stretches and, apart from bridge approaches, the rest was fairly flat. It was also 'open' for seven hours which was perfect for me.

In 2000, raising funds to buy Scotland's highest mountain for the John Muir Trust, I had walked from the Ben Nevis pub in Glasgow's Argyll Street to the top of Ben Nevis – a sort of West Highland Way with knobs on! Based on that experience, I knew that if the worst came to the worst, I could walk twenty-six miles in seven hours.

My marathon idea was almost ready to take to the editor. Bob Shields and Gordon Ramsay running the New York Marathon – for charity of course. Lots of features on diet, fitness and training on the build up to the big day. Then all the drama of the marathon itself.

You couldn't do better that 'Ramsay and Shields run New York' ... . unless you got 'Ramsay, Shields and McCoist run New York!'

I had written several features involving Super Ally over the years and we had got to know each other quite well. He had visited my home in Aviemore several times and we even bought a share in a local boozer together, The Old Bridge Inn, a cosy, fireside pub on the banks of the River Spey.

Alistair's popularity was limitless and he'd bring extra interest and no doubt a few laughs to the serious matter of running twenty-six-and-a-bit miles. The way I saw it, it would be an extra incentive to keep running, knowing that an almighty Big Apple piss-up with Coisty and Gordon was waiting across the finishing line.

The super chef had still to confirm, and Super Ally hadn't even been approached, but I took the idea to the editor anyway. I'd look a right diddy if I'd got my celebrities signed up – only for the boss to piss on the project from a great height.

And piss he did … he pissed himself laughing. 'You? Run a f****g marathon?' he said from somewhere underneath his desk. The boss had run a marathon himself, so he knew what I was letting myself in for. But he gave it the thumbs up.

There's an old saying that when one door shuts, another one opens. The journalistic equivalent is that when someone gives you the thumbs up – there's a guy around the corner is waiting with his thumb down.

The guy around my corner was, sadly, Alistair. Ally felt that his television obligations would limit his opportunity to fully commit to the training required. And with monies for charity at stake – not to mention his image – he didn't want to get involved in something where he couldn't guarantee his maximum effort. This was typical Coisty – 100% or nothing. He was absolutely right.

To be honest, I thought a man who had trained almost daily for most of his adult life would be in a good enough condition to sail through a marathon. But this theory was shot down in flames during a pint with Bobby Williamson, the ex-Ranger and manager of Kilmarnock, Hibs and Plymouth.

He explained that professional footballers trained for a specific physical role – short bursts of speed, turning, sprinting and jumping. The long haul of a marathon would be alien to most footballers. He also reckoned that most retired players had some kind of knee damage. And three or four hours of street pounding could be risky.

Bobby's assessment might have explained one of the reason's behind Alistair's decision – but it didn't fill me with any confidence.

I hadn't done any bursts of speed, not even wee tiny ones. To be honest, I hadn't done any f****g speed at all for over thirty years. If a marathon was 'alien' to most fit footballers, then smoking, drinking, overweight Shields was from another time dimension! What kind of shit had I got myself into?

The New York Marathon was now about seven months away, and I busied myself with finding out as much about it – and about marathon running in general – as possible.

The New York event is organised by the New York Runners Club and their web site includes an amazing 'virtual' marathon, featuring all the landmarks and points of interest on the twenty-six miles route.

Would I really be running across the two-tier Brooklyn Bridge I'd seen in a hundred movies? How would it feel to be jogging along the famous Fifth Avenue, or through the infamous Bronx? And would I make it to that magnificent green oasis in a desert of skyscrapers – the finishing line in Central Park?

On car journeys north to my Aviemore home, I began looking at road signs and tried to gauge what twenty-six miles really looked like. Could I really run from Glasgow to Stirling? Or from Dalwhinnie to Aviemore?

This marathon thing was becoming all consuming, and I hadn't started any proper training yet. It also took my mind off the fact I hadn't heard from Gordon for a while. To be honest, I was probably avoiding contacting him.

His name was featuring almost daily in the newspapers. He was now the star of a television show and was opening new businesses in London and Dubai. I knew he meant well by accepting my marathon challenge but reality was beginning to set in.

Taking Gordon out of commission for at least five days, to run a marathon, was looking less and less likely. I finally put myself out of my misery by contacting him and, sure enough, he was due to open a new venture the very same weekend as the New York race. He was very apologetic. Me? I was very much on my own.

At this point, I thought the editor might pull the plug on the whole project which, to be fair, wasn't half the package I had sold him. But to his credit, he didn't. What I didn't know was that he already had someone in mind to fill one of the empty slots left by Ally and Gordon. Himself!

Spring had now slid into summer and I had still to start any form of training. I kept putting it off until 'next week', and when next week arrived, I'd find some excuse to put it off for another seven days.

I finally decided that my annual holiday in Ibiza in late June would be the place to begin in earnest. Lots of sunshine, plenty of beaches to jog along and a swimming pool, yards from my hotel room door, to cool off in. Yes, two weeks of that and I'd come back tanned, lean, fit and ready to start knocking off the road miles back home.

But did I run up any mountains? No ... just a great big Bacardi bill. I was kidding myself on again.

And promising to cut back on the fags and booze on my return was another kid on.

News of my marathon attempt had leaked out to my boozing buddies in the *Daily Record* pub, the Copy Cat. No quarter is asked for or given in this drinking school and the first time I ordered a fresh orange and soda, they gave me pelters.

I stuck it out for a week or so, but my heart wasn't in it. For some reason, the jokes, the slaggings and the wind-ups that are part of Copy Cat life just weren't as funny with a soft drink in your hand. I went through a 'Bloody Mary' phase, telling myself that the vodka and tomato juice would be better for me than my normal rum and Cokes and Guinness. It was just another kid on. And it gave me heartburn.

But there was one memorable moment when a soft drink worked a treat. I'd been almost back to 'normal' drinking for a few weeks but, for some reason, I walked into the Cat one night and decided I'd open the session with a thirst quenching orange and soda.

No sooner had bar boss Billy handed it over when the editor made one of his very rare appearances through the door. He stopped and stared at my glass.

'F**k me, its Shieldsy drinking orange juice! Christ, you must be taking this marathon seriously right enough ....'

'My body is a temple, boss,' I smiled, and the rest of the pub hid their grins behind their pints.

He finished his drink and no sooner had the door shut behind him when Billy shouted,

'So it'll be a Guinness then, Big Boab?' The place fell about laughing. It was the best soft drink I'd ever bought.

On the positive side, I had stepped up my training. Honest! Green's fitness centre in Finnieston had given me free use of their facilities and I started attending most mornings. I'd set the running machine to a modest pace and keep going until I became breathless. Then I'd slow down to walking pace, get my breath back, and start running again.

Up in Aviemore at weekends, I embarked on a series of hour long runs – mostly in the direction of a tiny pub called The Souie. I devised a system of running for an hour, then having my partner Fiona pick me up in her car with the trip meter running. It was encouraging to see my 'hour' jump from five miles to almost eight after just two or three weeks in the gym.

With about twelve weeks to go before race day, the *Daily Record* finally trumpeted my marathon attempt – and launched the charity appeal that came with it.

I'd be running on behalf of Save Our Kids, the *Daily Record*'s own fund to build and staff help centres for children who had fallen victim to bullying.

My phone suddenly went into melt down. Lots of calls were from colleagues and friends whose messages were divided between, 'well done, good luck' and 'you're off you're f*****g head'. By lunchtime, 'you're off your f*****g head' was well in front.

But one of the more positive calls came from Sir Jimmy Saville, a veteran of 200 marathons, who wished me well and made the first donation to my marathon appeal.

And another came from Glasgow's Next Generation Health Club who offered to kit me out in the best Nike Pegasus shoes after a session on their new running analysis machine. I took up their offer and my old Adidas gutties were consigned to the bin.

There were now about eight weeks to go and there was another flurry of excitement when my 'race pack' and running bib arrived. By amazing co-incidence, the New York organisers had issued me with my old lucky number … 36907!

I went back into their web-site to check out details of bus routes to the start line and discovered some top athlete had written a complete preparation guide to marathon running.

'With eight weeks to go, all the hard work and the big mileage will be behind you,' he wrote. Behind me! Who is the f*****g joker kidding. I had still to venture into the 'no-man's-land' of big mileage – and I mean double figures! It was time to step up a gear and give myself a real test.

The next Sunday, in Glasgow, I decided to adapt my Aviemore 'hour runs' into a three-hour distance test. I was hoping for six miles in the first hour, five in the second and four miles in the last hour – a total of fifteen miles and well past the marathon halfway point.

Off I went and, with my shiny new Nike Pegasus shoes winging me forward, I felt quite comfortable. I left Glasgow's Queen Margaret Drive and trotted along Great Western Road, heading for Milngavie and the west. Running in the city for the first time, away from the running machine and the country roads of the Spey Valley, I had a new 'toy' to play with. Lamp posts!

I tried all sorts of little tactics – run past thirty lamp posts, then walk past five to get some breath back. Run past fifty and the walk ten, run past sixty and walk fifteen.

I had no idea how the great African distance runners prepared for their epic runs – but you can bet this wasn't it.

And before I could work out which strategy suited me best, I had disappeared into the countryside and run out of friggin' lamp posts!

After about two-and-a-half hours, I called Fiona and told her my route. Desperate to impress, I put on a final surge, knowing every stride would add something to the mileage gauge in her car.

She finally pulled up beside me, not far beyond the Glengoyne Distillery and near a pub called the Cherry Tree. If only I'd started my run at 10.00am instead of 7.00am, the boozer would be open by now! I climbed into the car and Fiona checked the mileage – I'd run sixteen point seven miles!

I still felt quite good and knew I could have kept going. I reckoned I could even have walked another ten and completed the magical twenty-six mile mark. After a long bath at home, I was in the pub at 12.30pm sharp for a celebratory Guinness or three. With seven weeks to go, the New York Marathon was suddenly looking achievable!

They say pride comes before a fall, and whoever 'they' are, got it spot on. The next morning I climbed out of bed … and fell over. My right knee wouldn't even support my body weight. It felt like someone had lifted out my kneecap, stuffed some broken glass inside, and closed it up again.

I hobbled through the rest of the day on pain-killers, and it eased slightly. Same again the next day. But the awful truth was that I couldn't even run between TWO lamp posts. Probably not even the length of a lamp post. The marathon date was six weeks on Sunday – and Big Bob was in big trouble.

I knew I needed medical help – and not the local doctor telling me to rest and keep taking the pills.

The *Daily Record*'s fund-raising juggernaut was picking up speed daily – there were tens of thousands of pounds resting on this knee. After months of worrying if I'd ever cross the finish line, I was now gravely concerned about even getting to the starting line.

I needed someone who knew about sports injuries, and how to fix them fast. It was time to get that battered contacts book out again and look up under 'G' … for Glasgow Rangers.

I could never claim club chairman David Murray was a best pal, but he wasn't a total stranger either. Our paths had crossed several times and I like to think he saw me as a journalist he could trust. And let's not forget, underneath that pin-stripped business suit is a fellow Ayr United fan trying to get out!

I made a call to Ibrox, explained my circumstances and asked if one of their medical staff could take a look at my knee. I didn't speak to David directly – that was 'Plan B' if some jobsworth told me to bugger off.

With the recently opened Murray Park as heavily guarded as Old Derry's walls, my guess was that such a request would have to go all the way to the top – and that the charitably disposed chairman would rubber stamp his approval.

Within twenty-four hours I had an afternoon appointment to see Dr Gert Jan Goudswaard, the Mr Fixit of the Murray Park treatment room. Out of respect – or was it fear? – I didn't touch a single fag all the next morning. I didn't want this respected sports injury expert to think he was wasting his time.

Again, this was another case of kidding myself on. He would only need a cursory glance at my ample belly and non-existent leg musculature to know I was the most unfit specimen ever to darken his surgery door.

A *Daily Record* photographer, recording my marathon build up for posterity, didn't even get as far as that.

'We've never done this for anyone outside the club before. You must have good connections ...' said the doc.

'Well ... Mr Murray is a very generous man,' I blustered.

'But if the public know we have done this for you, we'll get a stampede of injured charity runners. I must insist on no publicity,' he added, looking at the disappointed cameraman. And my treatment there has since remained a secret ... until now.

As Dr Goudswaard asked me to strip to my boxer shorts and lie back on his examination table, I wondered how many famous names had been here before me. It occurred to me that whole careers might have been ended by decisions taken in this very room. I was scared that my marathon dream was about to end here as well.

The doctor lifted my foot and turned my leg in all kind of directions. I felt a few mild twinges. Then he got his thumb and placed it firmly in a pre-determined spot. I jumped a foot in the air.

'Ah, just I thought,' he muttered.

He asked me to get up and walk up and down the treatment room floor. I hobbled about as manfully as my knee would let me.

'Your are a cripple, you know that?' he said in a crisp, Dutch accent.

'Well, I have felt better ...' I offered back.

'How long until this marathon?'

'Six weeks, doctor.'

'Six weeks! Then we have much work to do!'

He got out a plastic model of a knee joint and tried to explain what was wrong with mine. It was all a bit confusing – but the bottom line was that each knee has a bit that should go up and down. My bit was going side to side.

He went on to explain that my feet would need to be 're-balanced' in much the same way a car gets its wheels re-aligned.

'I am sending you to the Southern General's Department of Podiatry. They will make plaster casts of your feet and fit you with special insoles that should help your balance.'

He asked my shoe size, disappeared for a few minutes, and then returned with a pair of insoles that looked slightly the worse for wear.

'These are Arthur Numan's, but they should help for now. Wear them in your ordinary shoes and come back and see me next week. Meanwhile, rest, no running and take these anti-inflammatory pills.'

I made my grateful farewells and was halfway down the Murray Park hallway when the doctor called after me.

'Hey, Bob, I think Arthur will want them back!'

After my smelly feet have been in them? I don't think so!

I got my specially cast insoles the following week. In fact, they gave me a 'hard' and a 'soft' pair to test out. I preferred the more solid ones and kept the 'softies' as a reserve.

I returned to Murray Park several times and there was a noticeable improvement on every visit. But I still hadn't run an inch in almost three weeks – and there were just three weeks left.

But I kept the injury largely to myself. Those unforgiving mates of mine in The Cat would accuse me of getting my excuse for failure in early. And I didn't want to put off any potential sponsors.

Brewers Scottish and Newcastle had offered £1000 if they could put the name 'McEwans' on my running shirt. Very apt, I thought, because they were partly responsible for the shape of the body inside it.

And Howie Nicklesby of 21st Century Kilts in Edinburgh came up with the very first purposely designed 'marathon' kilt – a lightweight version with Velcro® straps.

As for the sporran, I didn't fancy the idea of a proper one flapping against my dangly bits for twenty-six miles. So I took an actual size photograph or my favourite 'hairy handbag' and had it laminated. It was perfect – almost weightless, but from just a few feet away, it looked like the real thing.

But the knee problem, though much improved, still gnawed away at my confidence. I needed something to lift me and rekindle my enthusiasm.

Out of the blue, I got it.

I received a call from Gary Ralston, a former *Record* man who had moved on to become the press officer for the Scottish Claymores, the sadly now defunct American football team. On the plus side, Gary is now back on the *Record* sports team.

Gary had noticed that the *Daily Record*'s anti-bullying campaign was almost identical to a community initiative set up by the Claymores. And one of its most committed participants was a defensive guard called Ian Allen, now with the New York Giants.

Gary, God bless him, thought the New York link between The Giants and the marathon was too good to miss. He wanted to take me over for a few days, 'train' with The Giants, interview Ian and hopefully give the Claymores some favourable publicity.

It would also give me a chance to look at the course and research some marathon-linked features for the weeks ahead. Well, that's what I told the editor anyway!

We jetted off and quickly settled into the Metropolitan Hotel on Lexington Avenue – before getting down to some serious 'researching' … where to get the best Guinness in town!

I discovered our hotel was famous for two reasons. Former Irish prime minister Eamon de Valera was born in a room there. And the subway ventilator outside the front door was where Marilyn Monroe posed for that famous photograph of the wind blowing up her skirt.

I tried the same trick with my new lightweight kilt – to no avail. But a nice young man thought I looked 'cute' and offered to buy me a drink at The Divine Club around the corner.

The next day we headed out to Giants' stadium, across the River Hudson at a place called East Rutherford, New Jersey. General manager Ernie Accorsi welcomed me with a Giants No. 1 jersey with 'SHIELDS' on the back. Then we went to meet the team at a huge indoor practice facility.

My 'training' included a few sprints with the players. A soccer equivalent would be going to Madrid and getting to train with Beckham, Ronaldo and Roberto Carlos.

This was just a warm down for the pros. For my legs, it was a shut down.

'Hey man, what day you startin' this marathon?' asked one player.

'A week on Sunday,' I told him.

'And what day you plannin' on finishin'?' he laughed.

But I interviewed Ian Allen and got the job done. And went to look at parts of the course as planned. I even put on my Nike Pegasus and took them to Central Park.

'Shoes, I want you to meet Mr Finishing Line. Mr Finishing Line, I'd like you to meet my shoes. You'll be seeing each other again real soon!'

It was a fantastic trip and a real morale booster. I'll never be able to thank Gary enough.

By now I was back in running mode, but not for any great distance. The insoles were a great help and Doc Goudswaard was very encouraging. On the day before I was due to fly back to New York for the race, I paid him my final visit and asked for his fitness verdict. I deliberately forgot to hand back Arthur Numan's insoles. Somebody, somewhere, some day, would be daft to enough to give me a tenner for them on eBay.

The doc was to the point. 'Bob, this knee could last six hundred yards, six miles, sixteen miles or all twenty-six miles. But, hey, good luck anyway!'

At Heathrow the next day, I met up with the editor and the second race replacement, Radio Clyde reporter Sara O'Flaherty who has moved on to sports presenting.

Sara is a smart cookie and a good looker alright, but I quickly discovered she carried some heavyweight boyfriend baggage. The dream ten months ago was boarding this flight with Gordon Ramsay and Ally McCoist.

Now, here I was, with a boss who had eyes in the back of his head and a girl who mentioned her fiancé and her forthcoming wedding at least once between breaths. But I couldn't have been happier. I was going to run the New York Marathon.

Or I hoped I was.

3

The New York Marathon –
Getting to the Finishing Line!

THE New York Marathon – two days to go. Our hotel, the Mayflower next to Central Park, was full of fellow runners. Across the road in the park itself, hundreds of people were stretching and jogging.

I didn't really grasp the enormity of the event until we went to race registration at the Jacob Javits Centre, a giant exhibition hall on the East Side, the next day.

It was packed with people and a Disney-sized queue snaked out the door and halfway around the building.

Everyone looked leaner, fitter and faster than me – even the doormen! And out of 25,000 people waiting in line, I was the only one puffing away at a fag.

After ninety minutes of slowly shuffling forward, the queue split into a separate channel for 'International Athletes'. If only the lads in the Copy Cat could see this, they'd fall about laughing. Big Bob – International Athlete! When I left to a wonderfully boozy farewell, they were having a sweep as to which hospital I'd end up in. The bastards!

Registration was a formality, the highlight being issued with your 'race chip' – a little electronic device you fit to the laces of your racing shoe. As you pass over special mats on the route, it records your time. It also means you can't start the race, hop in a cab to Central Park and finish two hours later. Including a stop for a bar lunch. The race is virtually cheat proof – unless you pop your chip into another runner's pocket!

I was looking forward to Saturday night, when my partner Fiona and my two daughters, Laura and Lisa, would be joining me in New York. I thought they would enjoy the trip – and knowing they were at the finishing line might keep me going.

That evening, we were all invited to a high powered dinner at a posh restaurant. The boss had some important New York journalist friends, and some pretty high profile UK newspaper folk were there as well.

All the next morning's runners opted for soft drinks … except for you-know-who. There was some rather nice Chablis floating about and I reckoned that if I hadn't stopped drinking already, the night before the race wasn't going to make much difference.

One UK editor spotted my slurping and asked my editor if he really thought I could finish the race.

The boss, probably unaware I was listening, paid me a giant compliment and gave my confidence a huge boost.

'Shieldsy? Well, would YOU bet against him?'

Back at the hotel, I kissed my daughters good night. For months, I had listened to the grim jokes about collapsing and dying on the course. It was all in good fun. But I'd be telling a lie if said it didn't cross my mind as they disappeared, laughing, into their rooms.

Race morning. 5.00am. We were all meeting in reception at 6.00am for buses from Times Square to the start line on

Staten Island. First mistake. I'd set the alarm an hour ahead and it was really only 4.00am.

While Fiona dozed, I put on the TV in a little separate lounge and lit a cigarette.

Then I popped out to a news stand and brought back some coffee and muffins.

The streets were already buzzing with men and women in running shoes.

Getting to the start is a marathon in itself. A giant queue had formed for the buses and we waited over an hour. Some folks wanted pictures of me in my kilt. But I knew what I wanted. I had pledged I wouldn't bring my fags with me to the race. But right now, I'd have mugged Mayor Giuliani for a smoke.

The principle of the New York marathon is that you run through all five boroughs of the city – Staten Island, the Bronx, Manhattan, Brooklyn and Queens.

It's a bit of a con. You only run a few hundred yards on Staten Island before crossing the Verrazano-Narrows bridge to Brooklyn.

Different bib numbers have different marshalling areas, where you meet and are ushered to the start like military platoons. We were all in different zones, so we wished each other luck and went our separate ways.

It was now 8.00am, three hours until the start. The smarter guys had brought folding chairs, blankets, coffee and food. Helicopters from news channels hovered above. I had a thick sweater on but was still a bit shivery. It was barely one degree above freezing, but some other guys said the real blessing was that it wasn't raining. But the ground was cold and damp and there was nowhere to sit.

As eleven approached, our group got nearer the start. What I had to remember was that 36,906 people were due to head off before me. The race could be started thirty minutes before I crossed the start line – but the little chip on my shoe would take that into account.

A cannon fired from a nearby army base and there was a huge cheer. We were off ... well, the 'elite' runners had jumped out of their heated motor homes and were off.

Further down the food chain, runner 36907 had now been on his feet for five hours – save a forty-minute bus ride. We all pushed forward, anxious to get started. As the magic line approached, people fiddled with their watches. Some crossed themselves. But just one thought was going through my head, 'This is the moment you haven't trained for!'

I crossed the line at 11.13am and jogged gently. Suddenly, something snagged my feet and I almost fell over. Then I was snagged again ... and again. I quickly discovered that over the first mile or so, runners cast off their outer clothing, usually an old sweater or cheap fleece.

As the field spread out over the bridge, the road was thick with unwanted clothing.

'F**k me, it's like hurdling through an Oxfam shop,' I thought.

I crested the bridge and began the long descent into Dyker Heights, the first populated area. People were lining the streets and cheering us on.

I'd been told to put my first name on the front of my shirt, so people could call out to me personally – it certainly worked. 'Come on, Bawb!' or 'Go to it, Bawb!' rang out every few hundred yards. But it still seemed to take forever for that first 'mile' marker to appear.

Then I got to my first drinks station, and what a state it was in. Some 36,000 people had passed here before me, gulped some water or Gatorade®, and thrown their cups away. I crunched my way over a sea of plastic.

There are also special stations where guys hand out bananas, lollipops or even chewing gum. You grab anything you can to distract you from the monotonous pounding.

A few locals also bake muffins, make up juice drinks and set up tables by the roadside. But, being New York, we were warned that some of them might be 'spiked' with all kinds of shit. I felt sorry for the old ladies who had baked all weekend – but no one was stopping for some meat loaf or pizza.

To be frank, much of the race is a blur. My tactic of mixing running with walking was going well but I was too busy straining to see the next mile marker to take in much of the local scenery. But jazz bands were playing and local radio station reporters were scurrying alongside runners getting a quick interview.

Run, walk. Run, walk. Mile eight. Mile nine. Mile ten. Then your brain starts to play tricks – when the marker says 'eleven miles' – have you run eleven miles or just started mile eleven.

The Queensboro Bridge loomed up ahead – the link across the river to Manhattan – but it seemed to take forever to get near it. Ten minutes, twenty minutes of good running, and it still wasn't getting any closer.

I'd arranged to meet Fiona and my daughters at the other side – it was my first mental landmark. This was the 'Glengoyne Distillery' mark – my three hour target.

Finally, I began the long, slow incline up the bridge, it seemed to go on forever.

Then, at last, the downhill part. I was going to make my first landmark after all.

At the foot of the bridge, a freelance photographer hired by the *Daily Record* called out 'Bawb, I need you over here!' I slowed up and walked over.

'Just a few pictures of you. Can you just go over there and look towards me ...'

I was frustrated at his interruption – Fiona and the girls would be nearby – but I was here to do a job as well.

After a few snaps, he still wasn't satisfied. Some runners didn't realise they were getting in the way of his precious lens.

'Can we just wait until all these people are out the way?' he said.

'Yeah, why not wait until the race is f*****g over. Then you can have the whole street to yourself, ya f*****g idiot.' Marathon running is a stressful business, you know. I apologised to him later, of course.

He got the message and I was off running again, and sure enough, my private band of fans were waiting at the top of 6th Avenue.

Many spectators held out posters and placards with messages for friends or family taking part. My daughters, who always called me 'dod' instead of dad, for some reason long lost in time, were holding up my reserve 'softie' insoles.

They had written 'Go, Dod, Go' on them.

'Sorry, Dod, when we saw everyone else had banners, this was all we could think of,' they explained. As far as I was concerned, it was the best banner the New York marathon had ever seen.

Some hugs and kisses and I was off again. I had hit sixteen miles in three hours and ten minutes – and I might have been bang on schedule had it not been for my friend with the camera.

I jogged off down the Avenue feeling great. I was on time, had hit my first 'landmark' and was feeling good. Thinking back, I often wonder if I allowed my body to relax a little for the first time but – BANG! – my knee popped like a champagne cork.

I slowed down to walking speed for five or ten minutes, then tried to pick up some kind of pace again. But no, my knee was having none of it. I was just short of the 'eighteen mile' post – and three and a half hours into the race.

It was decision time. Do I try to run and get a reasonable finishing time, and maybe risk knackering the knee altogether? Or do I walk in, as best as I can, finish the race within the allotted recorded time ... and get my medal?

There was really no decision to make at all. Bob was walking home.

There is probably only one day in the year a man in a skirt can walk through the Bronx – but everyone was happy to shout their encouragement. At least I think that's what it was. My only disappointment was that the locals were now taking the water station home in supermarket trolleys.

At twenty-three miles, and approaching Central Park, I knew I would finish, even if I had to crawl home. When I hit the stretch outside the Plaza Hotel, it was getting dark. Then I saw Fiona and the girls waiting behind a barrier – some of the few spectators left.

Lisa maintains she knew it was me because she saw the streetlights glinting off my swaying, laminated sporran! I shouted I'd see them at the finish line.

I turned into Central Park and decided to attempt a last jog across the line – if only for the benefit of the automatic camera that snaps every finisher.

A smiling girl draped a medal around my neck and wrapped me in a sheet of tin foil. I had done it. I had f*****g well done it! I was so excited I forgot to check my finishing time – but later I was told it was five hours and forty minutes.

The hotel was just yards away and the girls were hovering outside waiting for me.

Big hugs all round, and because it was dark, they couldn't see their big brave Dod had a wee tear to himself.

Next stop, the hotel bar. It was packed with medal wearing runners, but most had showered, changed and were ready to go out for dinner. The boss had finished well ahead of me, so had Sara. It was a good result all round and everybody was pleased for everyone else.

I ordered a drink and lit a cigarette: I felt fantastic. I called the Copy Cat to pass on the news to the late night stragglers. They all seemed delighted as well.

Then I felt a shiver, then dizzy, then sick. I put my drink down and staggered out into the lobby and fell into a seat. Thankfully, someone in crowd was a doctor and he knew a case of shock when he saw one.

'Who is with the guy with kilt?' he shouted into the bar. This startled Fiona, who ran out to see what was happening. 'Get him some bananas, some chocolate. I'll get him some liquid. Hurry!'

The queasiness and dizziness passed after some sugar and liquid. Then the shakes set it – giant spasms of violent vibrations through my whole body.

'A bath and get him to bed,' said the doc.

I slept for nine hours without a blink. Then I surfaced to find Fiona on one side of the bed … and my medal dangling on the other.

I got up, stretched, and felt a little stiff. And I was starving. But after breakfast, I was raring to go. I'd promised myself the treat of a new leather jacket if I finished the race. And a Guinness for every mile. It was best to start with the jacket.

Then we all went on a 'Round Manhattan Cruise'.

The tour guide began with a special announcement. 'Let's have a big round of applause for young Kerry here – all the way from Vermont to run in yesterday's New York Marathon. Show 'em your medal, Kerry!'

Kerry duly obliged. Everyone on the boat cheered … well almost everyone.

Lisa tugged at my shirt and whispered 'But Dod, you ran it as well! Tell the man you ran it as well!'

'Ssshh,' I told her. 'It's only a medal, it's no big deal.'

Then I sneaked my hand under my shirt to touch mine. Just to make sure it was still there.

4

That's No Hand Grenade, It's My Smoker of the Year Award!

THE mantelpiece at Chateau Shields isn't exactly groaning with Pulitzer Prizes. If the truth be known, it isn't groaning with any f*****g prizes at all.

My last significant honour for services to the fourth estate was a Young Journalist of the Year award, back in the days when the Dead Sea was only feeling unwell.

It was a plaque presented by the late Sir Hugh Fraser – and sat above my parents' coal fireplace until the heat eventually melted the glue holding it together.

I think that award was trying to tell me something. Something like 'From now on Shields, it all starts falling apart ...' And I was only eighteen at the time!

My one consolation is that my dear old maw was still alive to attend the presentation at a posh luncheon in Glasgow. She got to wear her best coat, got a free meal – and got the train home to Ayr in time to tell the neighbours to watch out for 'ma boy' appearing on *Reporting Scotland*. That'll do for me.

Some thirty years on, I have now reconciled myself to being an award losing journalist.

But back in 2000, a 'gong' did finally appear with my name on it.

FOREST, the freedom to smoke lobby, anointed me with their Journalist of the Year title. Yes, I was so good at campaigning for the freedom to puff, it was made illegal just six years later.

Not that I gave a monkey's back then. I was to be flown to London, and a glittering award ceremony, to mingle with some of the most famous smokers in Britain.

Sadly, the most famous smoker FOREST could persuade to turn up was the telly chef, Antony Worrall Thompson. And over a glass of champagne or six, he confided to me that he'd actually chucked the dreaded weed just a few weeks before.

The bash was held at Little Havana, a posh London cigar bar. It was stoagies-a-go-go all night as we strutted around with cigars big enough to take an eye out in the next room.

FOREST director Simon Clark was kind enough to tell me early in the evening that I wouldn't be required to make an acceptance speech.

This was good news as Chef Antony and I had more or less rendered ourselves unable to speak at all.

When my big moment came, Simon said some very kind words about my articles supporting the freedom of choice for smokers.

The audience was largely London based media and PR people and I recall half the room giving me a generous round of applause while the other half muttered, 'Who the f**k is Bob Shields anyway?'

Finally, Simon opened a box to present me with my award – a silver cigarette lighter in the shape of a life-sized hand grenade, sitting on a little engraved plinth.

'Bob, long may you continue to throw your literary bombs at those who wish to take away our freedoms,' he said. Or something like that.

I spent the rest of the night basking in my glory and offering everyone – probably even the non-smokers as well – a light from my glistening new toy.

The next morning, Bob's napper was hangover central. The editor had given me permission to start a little later than usual but that still meant a morning flight from Gatwick. So I threw everything into my overnight bag and headed for the train.

Post the Twin Towers horror, and subsequent airport security restrictions, what I was about to do was unbelievably stupid.

But as I trundled to Gatwick with my fuzzy head, I didn't give a thought to the fact I had a 'hand grenade' tucked in a bag beside my sweaty socks.

Even when the check-in girl did the usual stuff about 'packing the bag yourself' – in my befuddled mind, my hand grenade was still just a cigarette lighter.

It wasn't until I approached the security scanner that I finally realised what was about to appear on the X-ray screen. But even then, I was sure a simple explanation would get me through.

Also influencing this decision making process was the knowledge that the air-side bars would be open. And suffering Bob needed a pint of the black reviving fluid big time.

Rather than go straight to the scanner, and probably hold up the queue, I went over to one of the uniformed security men standing nearby.

'Excuse me sir, but I have an item in my bag that may be problematical ... you see, I ...'

The man cut me dead. 'Well, just put it through the

scanner and we'll see,' he said tersely.

'But I think you should …'

'And I think you should put it in the scanner – NOW!' he said.

So I joined the queue and when my turn came, watched my little bag disappear along the conveyor belt.

I don't how if the staff press an alarm button in these situations, but within seconds I felt a vice-like grip on my arm as a man dragged me out of the queue.

He was quickly joined by another man, also in plain clothes, who grabbed the other arm. They pushed me against the nearest wall and ordered me to put my arms out. Within another few seconds, they had patted me down and emptied my pockets – phone, fags, wallet, coins, the lot – into a polythene bag.

Then it was the frog-march to a windowless interview room with a table and a few metal chairs. The men left and an armed, uniformed officer was posted in the room with me.

To my shame, my opening line to the policeman was pretty pathetic.

'I can explain everything …'

'Well, you can explain it all to the investigating officer when he returns …' he replied.

Ten minutes later, a red-faced man appeared with my award in a plastic bag, my personal items in another, and my bag. He put them on the table, sat down and stared at me for an uncomfortable few seconds.

'Mr Shields – do you realise the seriousness of what you've just done?' he asked.

'I think once I've explained myself, it won't be that serious,' I offered.

'So how do you explain taking a f****g hand grenade on a passenger jet?' he said angrily.

'Well, let's establish right away that it's not a hand grenade, it's a cigarette lighter ...'

This implication that my interrogator was a total diddy wasn't well received.

'Yes, I KNOW it's a f*****g lighter, but the passengers and crew wouldn't know that if you threatened them with it ...'

'Do you honestly think that was my intention?'

He seemed to calm down a bit.

'Mr Shields – you have two minutes to convince me why I shouldn't arrest and charge you with offences under the Terrorism Act.'

I have to say that the words 'charge' and 'Terrorism Act' can have a remarkably sobering effect when you're stuck in an airport interview room.

To be fair, he listened quietly as I took him through the whole award ceremony and the symbolism of the 'hand grenade'.

I showed him my press card and my invitation to the party at Little Havana.

'What was I supposed to do – dump it in a litter bin? If you'd spotted that on your cameras you'd have shut the whole f*****g airport down,' was my closing line.

The officer nodded and thought for a few seconds.

'You could have posted it to yourself,' he said.

'Great idea! Let's do it now and the matter is resolved,' I said.

'No, Mr Shields, I think we will be confiscating your little trinket. In the meantime, I take it you have an editor who can confirm all this?'

Holy shit! No ... not the f*****g editor! When I thought of the boss being told I had marched into Gatwick with a 'hand grenade' – being charged under the Terrorism Act suddenly wasn't so bad after all!

'Yes – of course,' I mumbled, and began looking for a pen to write down the boss's direct number.

The officer picked up my boarding card, then checked his watch.

'Listen, Mr Shields, I'm going to let you walk out of here and you'll still catch your flight. I believe you made an unfortunate error of judgement here and that my staff acted fairly and reasonably. Would you agree?'

'Yes, I've been very stupid – and your staff acted very responsibly. It's good to know our airports are in safe hands,' I said, with my tongue firmly up my interrogator's arse.

He stood up and handed me my boarding card.

'Maybe that will be reflected in one of your articles one day?' he smiled.

'Indeed it might,' I said, stuffing my pockets with my telephone and wallet. The uniformed guy opened the door and escorted me back to the departures hall.

I checked the monitors and discovered my flight had been delayed by forty-five minutes. By my calculations, that amounted to a pint of Guinness and two Bacardi and Cokes.

Back in Glasgow, I slinked into the office just before lunch time. The first call I made was to Simon at FOREST who laughed his head off and promised me another 'hand grenade' would be in the post.

With uncanny timing, the boss stuck his head around the door.

'Ah, Mr Award Winner has finally graced us with his presence.'

'So, where is it?'

'Where's what?'

'Your award.'

'It's being engraved. Get it next week.' Well, it was only half a lie.

'What did they give you? A nice plaque or something?'
'No, a cigarette lighter.'
'Eh? That's not very f*****g exciting.'
'No, boss.'

Picture: A passer by!

Who's that gnarled old boozer with Richard Harris?
Taking a sip of the black throat charmer in London with the late and great actor Richard Harris. What was meant to be a sedate hotel room interview turned into quite a session – and he's proudly wearing the little Guinness lapel badge I gave him.

Picture: Ian Torrance

No escape for Ronnie Biggs in Rio …
The 'Great Train Robber' told me he was a great lover of Scots – for some very unusual reasons! But our meeting in a gay bar in Rio was one of my most memorable interviews.

Picture: George Hunter

You tell me your hairdresser and I tell you mine …
What a couple of scruffs … and that's how we looked before we went to the pub!
Oliver Reed ripped the sleeves of the rugby shirt I'd brought him – but he was a
perfect host when we had six pints for breakfast at his Irish local the next day.

Picture: Bill Fleming

An Olympic medal … for stupidity!
The Olympic Stadium in Atlanta was sealed off when we arrived – so we broke in through a fence to take this picture. What I'm staring at is an armed guard ready to open fire! We didn't hang about after that.

Pictures: Dan Callister

Running through the Bronx – in a skirt!
Well, there's only one day in the year anyone attempts that! That's me struggling along after about ten miles … but it's all smiles when I get that medal. Notice how dark it was when I finally crossed the finishing line (inset).

Pictures: Bill Fleming

And the Oscar for 'Best Tartan Scarf' goes to ...
*Is that for me? A slightly blootered Mel Gibson accepts my tartan gift after the
Oscar ceremony in Hollywood. His* Braveheart *movie got five Oscars that night –
and I helped get these exclusive pictures which made page one the next day.*

Picture: Bill Fleming

Hannibal Lecter I presume …?
At a pre-Oscar party in Hollywood, I got to interview acting legend Sir Anthony Hopkins – but he ended up interviewing me about the Bruno v Tyson heavyweight championship. Sir Anthony had great presence – and those Hannibal Lecter eyes scared the shit out of me!

Picture: Tony Nicoletti

Santa Claus is coming to town …
It started with a pub conversation
in Aviemore – and ended with me
handing out parcels to our troops
in Iraq. I was only in the country
three days before Saddam
gave himself up.

Picture: Ian Torrance

Tartan Amy on the move … by camel!
My four legged friend was absolutely
honking – but he did wear the scarf and
bunnet just like we wanted him to! This
trip to Morocco was part of my 1998 warm
up for the World Cup finals in France.

Picture: Alan Peebles

Did you have a nice flight, sir …?
The before and after … of a trip in a RAF
Jaguar jet. That 'Top Gun' feeling quickly
disappeared when we hit the sky. I can't say
I recommend being sick at 700 mph!

Pictures: Craig Halkett

I got a right kicking in Kansas from Mo-Jo …
With Maurice Johnstone and Richard Gough at a 'media day' with the Kansas City
Wizards. Mo-Jo put the boot in during a shoot-out – maybe it was that Ayr
United top I was wearing!

5

Grumpy Gavin Hastings – and the Day I Broke into the Olympic Stadium!

TODAY'S budget conscious editors have their own version of 'killing two birds with one stone' – and that's getting two feature articles for the price of one expense account.

The principle is pretty basic. If you are going to fly a journalist thousands of miles for a story, what's an extra 100 miles to come back with two stories. OK.

So you want an example?

In 1996, I was sent to a place called Carroltown, in Georgia, to look in on the pre-season training camp of the Scottish Claymores American football team.

With the help of a few million NFL dollars, the game was catching on in Europe and in Scotland. But the Claymores had grabbed the headlines with the sensational signing of rugby union legend and former Scotland captain, Gavin Hastings.

Like most editors, the boss had the headline, photographs and story in his head before photographer Bill Fleming and I had even got on the plane.

No one had seen Gavin in his American football gear. The boss wanted a page one picture of the full-back hidden inside his padding and helmet. The teasing headline would be 'Who is this famous Scot?'

Then the reader would be invited to turn to pages whatever and see Gavin unmasked – along with my exclusive interview. The 'job' had been arranged with the help of the Claymores' very pro-active press people – and it was exclusive to us.

This was going to be a scoosh. We'd fly, drive, sleep, wake up and knock off our Hastings exclusive before lunch. By mid afternoon I'd be at Augusta trying to blag my way onto the first tee at the home of The Masters!

The plan started to fall apart when we arrived at the Carrolltown camp – approximately three miles west of the middle of nowhere. Not even McDonald's had found this godforsaken spot.

But one other man had found it – a man with a couple of serious bits of Nikon dangling around his neck.

'Shit,' said Bill. And when Bill says a word like that, your anxiety level immediately goes to critical.

'Who is he?' I whispered.

At this level of operation, names are not important – just motives. Was he just some local football freak with a good taste in expensive cameras. Or was he the enemy?

'*The Scotsman* ...' said Bill.

It was my turn for the 'shit' word. The last thing we expected was a rival Scottish newspaper on the scene.

How long had he been here? What pictures had he taken? Had he filed yet? For all we knew, *Scotsman* readers from Berwick to Burntisland were already waking up to photos of Gavin in his new American football garb.

Our 'exclusive' could have already been booted into touch. And this would quickly be followed by more boots –

all aimed at the arse-end of Bill and Bob.

Bill gleaned what he could and it looked like we were safe. Our rival had arrived the night before – the word 'night' being all important. No one takes pictures in the dark – unless they have to of course.

However, his presence certainly raised the stakes. It was now 9.30am in Georgia – 3.30pm back in Daily Recordville ... and we had roughly three hours to shoot, write and send our words and pictures.

I had never met Gavin Hastings before but I was told he was usually polite and co-operative.

I was also aware that, of all Her Majesty's press in Scotland, the *Daily Record* probably wouldn't be the first one he picked up in the morning.

I greeted him with a bit of small talk about being tired after our flight.

'That's not my fault!' he snapped back.

Gavin clearly wasn't happy about something – and that something was probably us.

We wanted to do the helmet and uniform picture immediately – but Gavin wanted to do some more kicking. A Claymore official stepped in and explained that this was the picture we had been promised and his co-operation would be appreciated.

Gavin eventually obliged and put on his full kit – then gave me a reasonable if not scintillating interview.

Afterwards, I tried to think why Gavin was uneasy with us. I put it down to the notion that perhaps he was a little embarrassed about his new sport. I had always felt that Gavin was ten years too late in his career to cash in on his sporting gifts. The serious dough was coming in the dressing-room door just as Gavin was leaving it.

The Claymores contract was probably his final fling at some good money. Maybe Gavin felt that looking like a padded sofa in front of his rugby-playing peers would lead to the inevitable jibes in rugby club bars across the country.

It was only after I returned that it was revealed that Gavin's wife Diane was pregnant. Perhaps Gavin thought the *Record* had found out and that was the reason we were showing him such unusual attention.

I've never met him since to find out if either version is true. Then again, maybe he just didn't like me.

Anyway, we filed our story and pictures on deadline – and alerted our editors that *The Scotsman* was on the scene. They didn't need to be told that if they 'held' the story for another day, the exclusive element might be lost.

By late afternoon Georgia time, the *Daily Record* was printing with the 'Gavin Hastings exclusive' on pages one, six and seven – exactly the way the editor had planned it.

Telephone calls from late-night colleagues back in Scotland all had a 'job well done' theme to them. It was time for Bob and Bill to check out the local beers!

This little town had one steak house and we found ourselves some stools at the bar. The locals were in a corner, all staring up at a giant TV screen.

'What are they all watching?' asked Bill.

'Looks like the Weather Channel,' I said.

Over a few more beers, we learned that a tornado was hovering around the next state and was threatening to head next door to Georgia … and Carroltown.

Maybe it was the beer, but we were quite excited about the prospect. In my mind, I was already writing a gripping feature about being trapped at the heart of the storm. Bill had conjured up award-winning pictures of entire houses being sucked into the sky.

Every few minutes, the weatherman would update the tornado's predicted path. And every time he said 'moving away from Georgia' – the local folks cheered at the screen.

Well, what else could we do? Every time he said 'heading towards Georgia' – we cheered back.

The locals found this amusing – but the bartender didn't. This was maybe because he was, by now, the only person in the room who was completely sober!

'Guess you strangers never seen no tornado before,' he drawled as he dried a glass.

'No,' we replied in stereo.

'Well, Ah seen me plenty, boys. And if you had seen one, you wouldn't be sitting here all laughin' and grinnin' like that.'

He was probably right. We were behaving like a couple of diddies. But his remark suddenly took all the fun out of televised tornado tracking. We headed back to our motel where, thankfully, the three channels available in our rooms didn't include the Weather Channel – otherwise we'd have been up all night watching the damned thing!

Meanwhile, back at the *Daily Record*, a new day had dawned and a whole new paper had to be filled.

While we were sleeping, the boss was having one of his 'two stories for the price of one' moments.

The features editor called just after 8.00am.

The editor had seen something about the Olympic Games on TV. The 1996 Olympics were in Atlanta … and Atlanta was in Georgia … and, what a coincidence, we were in Georgia as well! With a day to spare before our flight out.

He wanted a 'Countdown to the Olympics' feature. You know, 'A Hundred Days to Go Until the Flame Is Lit – Our Man Bob Shields Is in Atlanta' etc. The picture he wanted was of me, sitting all alone in the heart of the stadium, surrounded by empty seats.

Where's a tornado when you need one?

But it wasn't the end of the world either. We had to take the car back to Atlanta anyway, and it might be quite interesting to check out the buzz at the host of the 1996 Olympiad.

Atlanta was also the home of Coca Cola – and I was looking forward to slamming the famous Cola into a very large Bacardi!

We drove down and hit the city about noon. There was no immediate deadline to this story – but we were flying out early the next morning. An afternoon in the city would be enough to get material and pictures, and we'd file our stuff the next day.

On most 'jobs', the pictures usually come first. The writer can do his bit from just about anywhere at any time – but the man with the camera has a host of limitations, not the least being the availability of his subject or even simply enough daylight.

We followed signs to the Olympic Stadium but we couldn't really miss it. There was building work everywhere and I began to wonder if they'd have everything finished in time. Perhaps that would be the story?

But as we approached the actual stadium itself, the amount of people working had almost vanished. A wire-link security fence had been placed around it, with occasional gaps for manned barriers to let essential vehicles in and out.

We parked up and approached one 'sentry' and asked him who we could talk to about taking some pictures.

'No chance. Maybe next week … I dunno …' was his answer.

But further conversation revealed that the stadium was in 'lock down'. A construction worker had been killed by falling concrete and the entire stadium evacuated until safety experts had completed their investigations.

The boss wasn't going to get his picture after all. No wonder Bill had another one of his 'shit' moments.

We drove around the curve of the outer stadium and out of sight of the security sentry. Bill parked and I lit a cigarette as we considered out options.

'What do you see, Bill?' I asked.

'A great big stadium surrounded by a great big f*****g fence!' he replied. He was obviously still in darkest 'shit' mood.

'And who is guarding this particular stretch of fence, Bill?'

He peered forward over the steering wheel, then arched back to check over his shoulder.

'There's nobody that I can ...'

Then a wry grin appeared across his face.

'Are you thinking what I think you're thinking?' he asked.

'Absolutely,' I replied. 'What's the worst case scenario? They catch us and boot us back out? Maybe even arrest us?'

'No,' said Bill calmly. 'The worst case scenario is that they shoot us! Did you see the size of that thing the sentry was packing?'

I lit another smoke and we stared out the windscreen. Then, suddenly, Bill jumped up and began grabbing at the cameras on the seat behind him.

'Big man ... I've just spotted a hole in our f*****g fence!.'

He was right. Two sections of fence didn't quite fit together and had left a man-sized gap. Behind that were two doors into the stadium, both wide open.

We jumped out the car and darted towards the fence – and then the door. Bill checked behind us, I was peering around the doorway with one eye. I hadn't done stuff like this since I pretended to be Ilya Kuryakin in *The Man from U.N.C.L.E.* TV series.

We were in a giant inner walkway, with stairs every fifty metres or so leading up to the seated area.

Bill would run up and check where we were in the relation to the picture he wanted – then run back down and say, 'Further!'

Finally, we found a stairway that suited his picture and he ordered me up.

We were slap in the middle of the main stand – it was an impressive stadium alright. I tried to imagine what it would be like when packed with 80,000 spectators.

Bill wanted me a couple of rows up and a few seats along, so I clambered over the seats – some so new that they were still in their polythene covers. I could imagine my foot-prints making wonderful evidence in some Atlanta courtroom.

Bill scuttled off down the stand, his cameras clattering off the seats as he went. Every few rows he would stop, check his viewfinder for a second, then clamber down a few more.

'Bill, for f**k's sake, just take the picture!' I tried to stage-whisper. But Bill hadn't gone this far to go back without the exact picture he wanted.

Finally, he was satisfied and trained his lens upwards to where I was, literally, a sitting target.

'Sit forward a bit ...' 'Look to your left ...' 'Move your right arm' – Bill went through all the usual photographers instructions.

But, unknown to him, an armed guard on the far side of the stadium was pointing at him and talking into his radio. Then another appeared ... this time a bit closer. Then another.

'Big man ... give us a smile!' shouted Bill.

'F**k the smiles, let's get out of here!' I shouted back, pointing behind him.

Bill turned, saw the guards and began running over the seats with the grace an Olympic hurdler would have been proud of.

We darted down the walkway and back out through the first door we came to. It was the wrong door and the hole in the fence and the car were still two hundred metres away. I honestly felt that, at any moment, I'd hear the crack of a gunshot and go tumbling to the ground.

We made it to the car, sweat dripping from our noses. Bill fired it up and we sped off down a side street. Then we dumped the car in an underground car park at the Sheraton Airport Hotel – just in case someone had clocked our number plate.

In the cold light of day – or rather over a cold Pina Colada in the Sheraton cocktail bar – we'd been absolute fools. All that risk for a picture that wasn't even particularly special, even though the boss had wanted it.

Would they have shot at us? We'll never know. But after the bomb attack in Atlanta just a few months later, they most certainly would have.

I've got a copy of the picture at home and it still makes me smile – and shiver – every time I see it.

6

Oliver Reed Had the Biggest Knob I've Ever Seen!

THE polished oak door at the front of the imposing mansion didn't have a bell to ring or even an intercom.

Instead, visitors announced their arrival by using the door knocker – a massive brass penis that swivelled on hinges attached to two equally impressive testicles.

I'd heard of a doorknob ... but this was taking the piss!

What kind of person lives in a house like this?

I give you ... Robert Oliver Reed.

And just getting to his front door was an adventure in itself, never mind getting past it.

The irrepressible Ollie had finished recording his latest film, *The Bruce*, in Scotland. The film's press people had offered me an exclusive interview with the acting legend, to publicise its premiere and launch in a few weeks' time.

Normally, these things would go fairly smoothly. But nothing was ever 'normal' when dealing with Ollie.

As Michael Parkinson famously found out, arranging an interview with Reed was one thing. Getting any sense out of him was quite another.

My interview had been arranged by his manager – aka Mrs Josephine Reed. A flurry of faxes had been exchanged between the film's publicists, Josephine and the *Daily Record* late on a Friday afternoon.

A time – 3.00pm – and a venue – Reed's Irish mansion house – had been agreed. Then suddenly, Josephine's fax machine went down. And equally suddenly, though not unexpectedly, the publicity people pissed off home for the weekend.

I had no address for Ollie – and my only method of contact was a dead fax machine.

'Don't worry, boss, I'll track him down if I have to go to every pub in Ireland!' I smiled at the editor.

'Shit. I'm worried already,' he groaned.

I searched the *Daily Record* cuttings library for any clues to the whereabouts of the Reed mansion. The clippings detailed every drunken episode of his hell-raising over the last two decades. But the only clue to his home was the repeated reference to a 'country mansion in Cork'.

This lack of basic information didn't go down too well with photographer George Hunter when I met him next morning at Glasgow Airport.

Snappers are a very methodical lot. They like to know the 'who, where and when' of every job. They also appreciate knowing where they are going to be wiring their pictures from.

All we had to go on was the 'who' and the 'when'. So when we finally touched down at Cork Airport around 11.30am – when had just over three hours to find the 'where'.

The first local we met was the head punter at Eire immigration control.

'Oi tink Ollie lives up to the north,' he said.

George and I got the map out. 'Well, that narrows it down a bit.' said George. 'The whole of f****g Ireland is to the north of Cork!'

Over at the Hertz Car Rental office, we fared a little better.

'Now then, I have family up near Mallow and they've seen him in the pubs up there. Tat's where I would start lookin',' he said, in a lovely Irish brogue. And so we did.

The beautiful little town of Mallow wasn't too far away and within the hour we were at the bar of the Hibernia Hotel – and my first chance to take a sip of the local Murphy's stout. Guinness it ain't but, hey, when in Rome … and we wanted to befriend the staff for some Ollie info.

'He was here yesterday, shopping with Josephine, he was,' said the barman.

'But, if it's his house you want, I'd go up to Churchtown. I tink he's livin' out tat way.'

Churchtown was barely a town at all. It had a church right enough, and a pub, but not much else.

We entered the pub, O'Brien's, and weren't exactly warmly received. I reckoned we weren't the first strangers to be poking around, asking about Oliver Reed.

The grey-haired barman shook his head. 'Rarely see him in here,' he said solemnly. But behind him, the gantry was covered in tattered Ollie photographs – including one with Ollie hugging the very same barman!

'We're not stalking him,' I pleaded. 'We're journalists from Scotland. His latest film is all about Robert the Bruce and Josephine has arranged an interview for three o'clock. If you call her, she'll confirm that. Tell her the *Daily Record* from Glasgow are asking directions for the house.'

My gamble was that Ollie would already have mentioned his filming in Scotland to his drinking buddies. And being open about our purpose, and inviting the pub to call Josephine, would all add to our credibility.

It worked. The barman relaxed as he poured us some beers and, within minutes, a local introduced himself and give us directions to the Reed home.

Only the Irish can give directions like the Irish. George and I quickly got lost among a warren of narrow country lanes with huge hedgerows on either side. But we found a smart driveway and followed it to a large, white country house with a bronze statue of a rhinoceros in the garden.

Any doubts we were in the wrong place quickly disappeared when we saw Ollie's impressive doorknob! But ominously, there were no cars outside the house and no sign of life inside.

I lifted the giant penis and knocked twice. Dogs began barking and after a few seconds, I heard the bolts being slipped behind the oak door.

The door opened and there was our man, unkempt, bleary eyed and obviously the worse for wear. Hey, I've been there myself ... but not at 2.45 on a Saturday afternoon.

'Good afternoon, Mr Reed. My name is ... '

'F**k off!' And Ollie slammed the door in our faces.

George and I walked back to the car, lit some cigarettes and weighed up our options.

Knocking the door again would only upset him even more. And we still hadn't seen the size of the dogs that lurked behind it. On the other hand, we did have an appointment and were here to publicise his latest film. We were the good guys, for f**k's sake!

George came up with the perfect plan. We would drop a note to Josephine through the door, saying we had arrived and could be contacted by mobile or at our hotel in Mallow.

The best part of this plan was that George got to check out the hotel phone lines for wiring any pictures. And if we had to play a waiting game, I would be doing it my favourite Saturday afternoon surroundings – a boozer with a telly.

On the down side ... what if Ollie's dogs liked eating notes?

But the problem was solved for us when a car appeared up the driveway and parked beside us. I had never met Josephine, but recognised her from many press photographs published over the years.

She was delighted to see us ... and a little embarrassed by our 'welcome' from her husband.

'Let me go and talk to him,' she said, and disappeared around the rear of the house.

She returned a few minutes later wearing a big smile. 'He was just a bit confused but he's fine now. Come on in ...'

We followed her to the kitchen entrance. Inside, a couple of strange looking locals were sitting around a big farmhouse table with some bottles of Paddy Power whiskey already opened.

'Some of Ollie's friends have dropped in ...' she smiled as she waved us through to a giant drawing room.

Oliver Reed was waiting for us with a maniacal grin on his face. His eyes were red and his hair flattened. I reckoned Ollie was not long out of bed and had just had a glass of Paddy Power for breakfast.

We all shook hands, Ollie doing his best to squeeze the life out of mine. He was a big bear of a man.

I began by handing him a present I'd bought the previous afternoon.

According to reports, Ollie was going to attend a Scotland v Ireland rugby match at Murrayfield before the premiere of *The Bruce*.

So I had brought him an official SRU Scotland top – XXL of course. 'Wonderful ... it's wonderful ... you're so kind,' he gushed.

Our relationship had certainly moved on since he told me to 'f**k off' barely thirty minutes ago.

After ripping the shirt out its bag, Ollie then ripped off his black sweater. He seemed to wrestle around in his new shirt forever before his big grinning face appeared through the collar.

Everyone was smiling and laughing ... until Ollie realised that his shirt had sleeves.

'What are these f*****g things? You don't wear sleeves in the scrum!' he thundered.

He ran off to the kitchen and returned with a dirty great big steak knife, then began hacking and slashing at the sleeves.

A half-pissed Oliver Reed swinging a knife around is bad enough – but I reckoned that if he wanted to cut the sleeves off his new jersey, it might be a good idea to remove his arms from inside them first!

Josephine clearly didn't fancy a one-armed husband either and ran off to fetch a pair of scissors.

Ollie drew a line across the top of his arms with a finger – and Josephine dutifully snipped away at the thick, dark blue cotton.

Just a few hours ago, I'd made a special effort to get to Greaves Sports in Glasgow to buy Ollie his special gift. Now my £42.99 present was in ragged bits. But the big man seemed pleased.

Then, suddenly, he charged at me like a raging bull. I'm not exactly a butcher's pencil, so I readied my sixteen stone to meet Ollie's run. Whack! In a blurred instant I was flat on the floor with a giggling Ollie sprawled on top.

'What a f*****g tackle! Eh? Now it's your turn to tackle me,' he laughed.

I'd never played much rugby. Certainly not one-a-side

and never against a semi-blootered international film star … in his own drawing room.

I looked at Josephine, obviously with enough panic in my eyes to make her intervene.

'Darling, Bob's here to talk about your new film – not wrestle around on the floor.'

'Wrestle? OK, let's wrestle,' he said.

Then he lay stomach down on the floor, balanced his elbow upright and offered me the classic arm-wrestling position. I glanced across to photographer George who was hopelessly trying to suppress a smile.

The look on his face said, 'Rugby shirt? That'll f****n' teach you, Shields …'

I got down and took Ollie's hand. At first, he repeated that life-extinguishing grip of his – it was agony. Then, slowly, he put his bulk behind his arm and I could feel mine start to wobble. I managed to hold off his first real push … but I crumbled like a meringue at the second.

'I thought a Jock would have put up a better fight than that!' he huffed. George was creasing himself. As Ollie disappeared to the kitchen, hopefully returning with a dirty big Guinness, I wiped the dog hair from my jacket.

'Aye, I let him win to keep him happy. But after we've got the interview – he's getting it!'

Ollie came back without a badly needed Guinness but with a bottle of Paddy Power and some glasses. The drawing-room-floor antics appeared to have sobered him up a bit and we drew up some chairs to get down to the serious business of the interview. Mind you, it was all a bit surreal considering Ollie was still dressed in his sawn-off rugby shirt.

We were doing very well and I was filling pages of notes with Ollie's thoughts on the movie, Scottish history and life in general.

There was no doubting that Mr Reed was a very well-read and extremely intelligent man who took his craft very seriously.

Then we were interrupted by a voice from a corner of Ollie's vast drawing room. 'Tat's one nil for United,' the voice said.

I paid no great attention as I had Ollie sober and talking sensibly. I didn't want any distractions.

But minutes later, the voice from the corner was a little louder and a little more excited.

'Hey, that's United two up. What a goal by Giggsy!'

I looked around the room and Ollie obviously agreed it was time to unveil the mystery voice.

'Show yourself, ya little f****r!' Ollie boomed.

And from behind an armchair, a little grey-haired head popped up. It was Alex 'Hurricane' Higgins, the former world snooker champion and a man whose legendary boozing was almost on a par with his host's.

I glanced across at George who began slowly stroking his camera the way a gunman fondles his Colt 45 before a Western saloon shoot-out.

Ollie introduced us and explained that Alex was a frequent house guest.

'He's a night animal,' he added. 'He sleeps all day, maybe watches some football, then he's up all night. I can't sleep for the noisy bastard Hoovering the f*****g floors at four in the morning!

'But Josephine loves him. She gets up to find the house is all tidy and the dishes are all washed.

'And sometimes, we'll go for a drink and play a bit of pool. We usually win a few bob, don't we, Alex?'

Higgins nooded sheepishly. 'If it's all the same to you, I'll get back to the football now ...' and he slipped back in his chair out of sight.

I looked at George, he looked at me ... but Ollie caught us looking at each other.

'I don't want anything about Alex in this story. He's here to rest,' he said, with some finality.

It was obvious a picture of Alex and Ollie together was going to be almost impossible. But George pointed to his camera and gave me a shrug. We'd been in Ollie's house for over an hour and he hadn't taken a single frame. My notebook was full – but his camera was empty. It was time to broach the subject of photographs.

'Ollie – can I just take a couple of shots while you talk to Bob?' George asked.

Ollie flew into an instant rage – it was like flicking a light switch on.

'Photographs? In my house? In MY f*****g HOUSE! You walk into a man's home and want to take photographs?'

Ollie's rage brought Josephine running from the kitchen. At least she hadn't brought the friggin' knife with her. I spotted Higgins peering over the top of his chair to see what was going to happen next.

'Ollie, we're doing a feature to publicise your new film. But without pictures, it's not going to get very far, is it? You have to understand ... '

Ollie, by now red faced, was having none if it.

'In MY home, the privacy of MY home!' he raged.

'Well, how about pictures away from your home?' asked George.

'That's a good idea,' smiled Josephine.

As quickly as he became angry, Ollie was almost calm again.

'Yes, yes ... I know the very shot. From the hill, overlooking the gardens ... with Josephine's horse ...'

'It's getting a bit dark,' added George.

'Tomorrow then, tomorrow morning at ten. Can you manage that?' asked Ollie.

'No problem, we will be here at ten sharp,' I agreed.

Ollie looked at George's cameras, then picked one up, peering out the window through the viewfinder. The thought of directing his own 'photo shoot' clearly appealed to him.

George gave him a few tips on adjusting the focus – soon they were chatting away about photography like two camera club amateurs. Then George seized the moment.

'Ollie, you look great in that rugby shirt. Can I just take one? Nothing in the background, no house, just a close-up of you and the shirt Bob kindly brought you.'

The less than subtle mention of my gift was clearly obvious.

'That would be nice,' added Josephine who was rapidly becoming an all-important part of oiling the proceedings.

'Yes, fine,' said Ollie. And he began posing in the sawn-off jersey like a circus strongman. George took as many as he thought he could get away with.

'Right, see you tomorrow at ten,' said Jospehine.

George and I drove off to our hotel back in Mallow. I had a great story – the appearance of Higgins was the icing on the cake.

But George had only one picture of any worth – Ollie in the rugby shirt. Exterior shots of his house we'd already taken, and even that outrageous doorknob, wouldn't cut it with the picture desk back in Glasgow.

The big fear was that Ollie would fail to turn up at ten the next morning. What if he changed his mind, slept in or arrived pissed out of his brains … with that friggin' knife in his hands?

That was tomorrow's problem.

But tonight would be spent in beautiful Ireland, home of the famous, black throat-charming fluid.

And that would be no problem at all.

7

Six Pints for Breakfast ...
then Ollie Wanted to Go for a
Drink!

MY hotel room was on the first floor, overlooking Mallow's quaint main street, and I woke to the sound of cheerful Irish voices wishing each other 'good morning'. It was 7.50am.

My first thought – that the pubs here opened early and the street throng was the first wave of Sunday boozers – turned out to be wishful thinking.

A glance out the window revealed everyone dressed in Sunday best and a few carrying bibles and flowers. My 'early boozers' were Sunday worshippers.

This was disappointing as a cold pint was exactly what was needed to kick-start my brain. The night before had been a good one with some traditional live music and 'craic' with the locals. And more than my fair share of the black stuff.

Some folks had told me their 'Ollie stories' – mostly about him getting steamboats while Josephine did the shopping. Like a dutiful journalist, I had jotted their tittle-tattle down in my notebook.

But when I glanced at the pages in the sober light of morning, they were indecipherable. I couldn't make out any of my shorthand squiggles – it looked like an order for three chow meins and an egg foo yung.

I followed the wonderful waft of frying Irish bacon down to the dinning room where George was heartily tucking into a full breakfast.

He had already checked in with the picture desk and told them what he had – and hadn't – got on film. Their reply was to ask George to get the best pictures he could during our morning 'shoot' and file them as quickly as possible.

'Do you think he'll show up?' asked George.

'I think Josephine will make him show up … but I've no idea what state he'll be in,' I offered.

We left the hotel in good time and parked at the foot of the Reed driveway for a smoke.

We didn't want to appear too early and risk pissing him off. Or arrive a few minutes late and give him the excuse to tell us to 'f**k off' again.

I rattled the giant penis at the stroke of ten precisely.

The oak door opened and Ollie emerged wearing a huge woollen camel coat and a pair of green wellies.

'Morning, lads – you've got a great day for your pictures!' he beamed, and took a huge lungful of the morning Irish air.

His eyes were a little red and I doubted his face had seen soap and water, or his hair a comb. But, hey, he was here and raring to go.

'George, I thought maybe one of me up on the hill, with the house in the background. The light is just perfect …'

'Whatever you think,' George nodded.

Here was a man who had spent his life in front of the cameras, with some of the best in the film business, now personally directing his own photo shoot. No wonder George was happy to go along.

We climbed over a fence and began trekking up the grassy hill. Barely two paces in, our feet were disappearing into what looked like a fertile mix of mud and cow shit.

'This explains his f*****g wellies,' I moaned.

'I always carry spare wellies in the car,' said George.

'Well, go and get them!' I suggested.

'The car's at Glasgow airport you dickhead,' he replied.

I guess I needed that Guinness kick-start to my brain more than I appreciated.

Halfway up the hill, Ollie made that square viewfinder shape that the movie people do with their hands.

'This will be perfect, George. I'll stand here, you stand there, the house will be visible over my left shoulder ...'

I was rapidly getting pissed off with Mr Reed. Yesterday, we were invading the privacy of his precious house. Today, he was serving it up on a sunlit f*****g plate. Trudging up to your knees in muddy shit wasn't helping the situation either. But George snapped away like the pro he is.

George asked if he could do one of Ollie and me together. He rattled off a few frames then decided the best picture would be the two of us facing each other. We squared up like a couple of gunslingers.

'Closer,' urged George. We moved a few paces.

'No ... closer still,' he insisted.

Finally, Ollie and I were standing nose to nose. Like a couple of schoolboys, we tried to stare each other out. His eyes were watery and pink – but he was probably thinking the same about mine.

From memory, I think I was the one who blinked first. I reckoned, if I didn't, Ollie was in the perfect position to 'nut' me on the nose.

But it made a great picture – and one than still sits proudly on the walls of Chateau Shields.

Suddenly, we were distracted by the clattering of hooves on the tarmac surrounding the Reed mansion.

'Aha! About bloody time!' roared Ollie, who went on to explain that a horse always added rustic charm to any scene. A bearded bloke, who I think was one of the 'friends' drinking whiskey in the kitchen the day before, led the grey nag towards us.

The horse didn't look too happy. But I suppose, if I were hauled out of a warm stable, then dragged up a hill to have eighteen-stone Oliver park his fat arse on me, I wouldn't be singing and dancing either.

What all this had to do with Ollie and his new movie was a mystery but, if the picture editor wanted something different, then a half-pished famous actor, in camel coat and green wellies, perched on a horse on an Irish hillside was it.

I grabbed a few more quotes from Ollie on our way back to the house and George was happy he'd got some pictures at last.

'Right – breakfast time,' announced Ollie. 'Would you lads like to join me?'

I had visions of us sitting in his kitchen with Josephine pouring tea as locally made black puddings sizzled on her Aga. Well, breakfast was black all right, but the only pudding turned out to be me.

The beardie leading the horse had now changed jobs from stablehand to chauffeur. He pulled up in a dirty Land Rover and Ollie jumped in.

'Just follow me,' he said and off they went.

We piled into the hired car and tailed them all the way to the village … and O'Brien's pub. It was barely 11.00am.

Ollie breezed in to a noisy welcome from the dozen or so boozers making an even earlier start than we were. Poor

George was driving and declined all offers of any alcohol whatsoever. But my tongue was drier than Gandhi's sandals – I was gagging for a Guinness.

Ollie kindly set them up and we 'clinked' our pint glasses. Here I was, sharing a quaff with one of the most famous drinkers on the planet. Marvellous.

I think I was on my second sip when Ollie slammed his empty glass down on the counter. Shit! 'Same again please,' I ordered, pulling some local punt notes out my pocket and gulping my Guinness to keep up.

We chatted and drank and drank and chatted. But mostly, we just drank. To Ollie, a pint was not much more than two gulps. In the space of twenty minutes, I was suddenly ordering up round number six.

George was manfully switching from orange juice to ginger beer and lime – and back again. When Ollie finally disappeared for a piss, I agreed with George that we'd try and make this one our last.

I was still trying to get a mental handle on the fact that I was about to leave a pub before friggin' OPENING time!

Ollie emerged from the toilet looking no worse for his six pints. In fact, he was looking better than he did when we went eyeball to eyeball half an hour ago!

'Right, lads, we're on the move!' he announced. Then he signalled to Beardie to finish what looked like a large whiskey.

'This is some country,' I thought to myself, 'Six pints before opening time and the chauffeur's on the f*****g piss as well!'

'Er ... where are we going?' I asked.

The big man flashed a grin that I last saw watching him swash his buckle in *The Four Musketeers*.

'Well, you've had breakfast – now we're going for a f*****g DRINK man!'

We followed him out and jumped in the car again. George and I now had a dilemma. This would be a good time to bale out and leave Ollie to it. We had a story to write and pictures to send.

But how often do you get the chance of a Sunday session with Oliver Reed? And who knows, maybe Ollie and Hurricane Higgins will get on the pool table? What a story that would make!

We decided on a 'suck it and see' policy. We would follow Ollie to his next boozer and make a decision after checking out who was there.

We arrived at a place called Liscarrol and another boozer. Ollie barged in and ordered up a large Bushmills Irish Whiskey.

'What's your malt?' he asked.

'I'll have a Bacardi and Coke thanks.'

I might as well have asked him for a night in his stable with Josephine.

'What! What kind of Scotsman are you? F*****g Bacardi?' he roared.

'It's what I drink – and if you won't buy it, I'll get my own f*****g drink,' I replied, obviously slightly emboldened by the previous glugs of Guinness.

'Och, give the Jock what he wants ...' he finally conceded, and stuffed a handful of notes in the barmaid's hand with obvious disgust.

It only took a sip to realise I might have got the drink I wanted – but I'd got the measure Ollie wanted. Six Guinnesses and now I was on large Bacardis. Holy shit.

By this time, poor George had given up orange juice and was munching packets of crisps. But the rounds kept coming – although I whispered to the barmaid to slip me normal measures when Ollie wasn't looking.

I was starting to run out of things to say to Ollie – not to mention gradually running out of the ability to say anything at all.

Six pints of Guinness and another half dozen rums is a fair shift in anyone's book. And the pubs had only been officially open ten minutes!

We decided to bid Ollie farewell and I got my last bone-crushing handshake, and a hug, from the big man.

As we drove back to the hotel, I decided I really liked Oliver Reed. But at the pace he was living, I knew that one day he'd just keel over and never get up again.

Back in Mallow, I needed a bowl of soup, an hour's nap and a shower before I was ready to start writing. George disappeared to his room to file his pictures. Thirty hours after arriving at Cork without even an address for Ollie – the job was finally done.

Three years later, I would be back in Mallow. My prediction that Ollie would one day keel over sadly came true.

There had been speculation that his funeral would be a star-studded event. Peter O'Toole, Richard Harris and Sean Connery were just some of the names running on the wires. As a journalist with some local knowledge, I was sent to record his send-off.

This time, Mallow was buzzing with press and TV crews … and the bars were buzzing with rumours.

George Clooney had been spotted leaving a private jet at Cork, Tom Cruise was arriving in Dublin and George Best had got blootered the night before at Liscarrol.

But on the day, the only famous face at his funeral was Alex 'Hurricane' Higgins. And he looked so gaunt and frail, you would have bet on his funeral being next.

Robert Oliver Reed was laid to rest in a pauper's cemetery in Churchtown on May 15 1999.

He chose the plot himself.

It's right behind his beloved O'Brien's pub.

8

The Iraqis Wouldn't Shoot
Santa, Would They?

IT was a Sunday afternoon in Aviemore and Hibs were playing live on the Cairngorm Hotel's giant TV screens. That combination of circumstances usually meant one thing was certain – George Gaff would be sitting at the bar.

Ginger George loves four things in life – his family, the 1st Battalion Royal Scots, Hibernian FC … and a swally. Today, he was enjoying two at the same time. But a third wasn't far from his thoughts.

When I joined him, he was in animated conversation with a couple of mates.

'Scandal. Absolute f*****g scandal!' he was saying.

'The Battalion, away for ANOTHER Christmas. Some of these laddies haven't had a Christmas at home for years. Put that in your paper, big man. F*****g scandalous!'

From experience, once George got excited, getting him to calm down was like getting a shit out of a clothes horse.

Further experience had taught me that, when Hibs triumph, George is on another planet. And if they happen to triumph over Heart of Midlothian, he's on another planet for a week!

So I pulled him aside before the match got underway. My instinct told me there was a good story here somewhere.

'George, who is going where?'

'The Battalion, going to f*****g Iraq in December. The boys just heard yesterday. It's no' right, big man …'

Having recently left the Battalion himself, George's concern was for the mates he used to eat beside, sleep beside and fight beside.

'Ah wish Ah going with them, big man … but they won't let me back … Ah miss the Battalion wi' a passion ….'

The actual invasion of Iraq was all but over, but this was still only 2003 and stories of British forces being deployed there were still big news.

'How many men, George?'

'Och, there's "A" Company and "C" Company – plus the 'Recce' lads …'

'George, don't talk Army, talk numbers for f**k's sake.'

'Oh aye … er … aboot 600, big man. Maybe a few more.'

'And mostly Jocks?'

'Aye, just about.'

'Has this been announced yet, George?' I asked. For all I knew, the story might have been all over the Sunday papers that I hadn't even opened yet.

'Hey … big man … it's probably still a bit "hush-hush". Don't do anything yet, let me make a few phone calls first.'

No problem. George got the pints up and we settled down to watch the Hibees. But I could tell his mind wasn't completely on the game. And to be honest, neither was mine.

Six hundred Scots, in Iraq, for Christmas? There had to be some great feature material in there somewhere. And maybe even a trip to Iraq to visit them.

Back at my Aviemore house, I picked up a *Sunday Mail*. Somehow, it jogged my memory of a charity campaign they had run a few years before. It involved filling shoe boxes with donations for kids.

That was it! Invite our own very generous army of *Daily Record* readers to fill Christmas boxes for the Jocks in Iraq.

The more I thought about it, the better I liked it. We could involve shops and businesses, clubs and pubs, schools and associations and ask them to donate their own boxes.

Hopefully, MPs would want to get involved as well – and perhaps a few celebrities. After barely half an hour, my notebook was filling with people we could ask to send the Jocks a box.

Then I realised I had a catchy name for the whole project – 'Send the Jocks a Box'! And who else could possibly go to Iraq to help hand over our Christmas parcels? Step forward – Santa Shields!

My idea suddenly had potential features oozing everywhere. I rattled off a basic proposal to show to the editor in Glasgow the next morning.

I knew I was on a winner before I even stepped into his office.

'Send the Jocks a Box' had all the right ingredients – huge human interest, a big Scottish element, community involvement, a dash of celebrity, a very worthy cause – and all wrapped up in Christmas paper, the season for 'feel-good' stories.

It was only when I left his office with the official 'go ahead' that I began to realise what I might have let myself in for.

But first things first – I had to get back to Ginger George to open a line of communication with the Scots Guards. For all I knew, they might tell Santa Shields to f**k off and don't be so silly!

But George did the business. The idea was quickly run up the Royal Scots' flagpole and got its salute. Within a day, I had Major Gene Maxwell on the telephone asking what he could do to help.

We arranged a meeting and, in true military style, a battle plan was drawn up. It would be my job to organise the campaign and get the boxes to the Battalion's barracks on the outskirts of Edinburgh.

It would be his job to get the boxes – and me and a photographer – to Iraq and into the army bases.

We also drew up a list of what would be allowed in the boxes – and what wouldn't. And sadly, top of the list of banned substances was bevvy. The poor bastards wouldn't be getting a Christmas swally. And even worse, neither would Santa!

We also agreed that, although the campaign would be centred around the Royal Scots, Santa's sack would be open to any UK servicemen in Iraq.

After the meeting, it did strike me that Major Maxwell had, literally, a battalion of people to help him. Santa Shields was on his 'Jack Jones'.

My first priority was finding a company, with nationwide branches, to agree to host collection points. I got lucky right away with Scotmid and Semi-Chem who, between them, had shops in most of Scotland's main towns and cities.

The campaign was launched on the back of a feature showing the Scots Guards training at Hereford – with personal interviews on how they felt about being away from their families and loved ones at Christmas.

A front page and a centre spread in the *Daily Record*, it touched the nation's heart just as I hoped.

The following day, the *Record* ran a second feature on what to put in your box, and a list of the collection points. 'Send the Jocks a Box' was go! And within days, it was starting to go out of control.

My phone was ringing off the hook with offers of help. But the bane of my life quickly became those readers who lived in towns or villages with no official collecting point.

Old ladies would call and say, 'Hello, son, I've got my box here ready for you. Aye ... in Plockton. Can you send a man round? But not until the afternoon because I've got Betty in the morning. Betty's my physiotherapist – it's my hips you see ...'

Well, you get the drift.

It was a flaw in my planning that couldn't be reasonably resolved.

Another major f**k-up was discovering halfway through the campaign that the boxes should not be wrapped but, for obvious security reasons, easy to open for inspection.

And by now, we had hundreds of boxes, many dutifully wrapped in Christmas paper and tied with ribbons. Oh shit!

On the upside, everyone from the Lord Provost of Edinburgh to the Chancellor of the Exchequer had donated a box. Hibs gave away match tickets to be used when the lads came home.

And generous staff at travel firm Direct Holidays donated over a hundred boxes. One of them contained a voucher for a holiday for two ... and another contained a pair of knickers from a cheeky girl in tele-sales. The *Record* was getting plenty of stories alright!

It all became much more meaningful when I was sent to cover the Scots Guards actually leaving for the Gulf. I had a serious lump in my throat as fathers hugged the children and kissed the wives they might not see for another six months. And then there was the stark reality that no one wanted to even think about ... that some of these men might never see their families again.

As December approached, Major Maxwell came on to report some bad news.

RAF flights in and out of Basra would be restricted at Christmas time. They would also be limited to essential items like supplies, water and all the other things a modern army needs to survive. And, of course, essential personnel as well.

Sadly, a shoebox containing macaroon bars, Irn-Bru and the *Rangers News* didn't qualify as essential items. And Private Santa Shields wasn't quite up there in brigadier class.

The photographer and I would have to go out around the 12th and return around the 18th – missing Christmas Day itself.

The best we could hope to do was to hand out the boxes early and 'hold' the story and pictures for a few days.

I had been really looking forward to reporting from the front on Christmas morning and joining the lads for their turkey and Christmas puds. But, as they say at that time of year, 'it's the thought that counts'.

Surely it couldn't get any worse? Oh yes it f*****g well could!

The Major was on the phone again and told us that on any flight, our 'non-essential' boxes might get shunted at the last minute for more urgent cargo.

This opened up the possible scenario of Santa Shields standing in the desert with an empty sack while his sleigh filled with goodies was parked in a shed in pissing England.

Aw ... for f***k's sake! What a disaster that would be.

And some people think I take a drink because I like the stuff!

This couldn't be allowed to happen. The whole object of the exercise was lots of happy snaps and words of comfort and joy as our boys opened their boxes.

Our fall-back plan was to take as many boxes as we could in our personal luggage. It might only be a few dozen but it would be enough for some pictures, and ... 'it's the thought that counts'.

But these were worst-case scenarios. Scotmid and Semi-Chem, not to mention hundreds of volunteers, carried on with the collection process.

December 12 approached and our boxes had made it to the Edinburgh barracks for scrutiny and then were driven down south to RAF Brize Norton in Oxfordshire for transport to Basra.

Santa Shields and his not-so-little helper, photographer Tony Nicoletti, were ready for take off. Bring it on, Saddam!

But not before I had to do my own farewells to my partner Fiona and my daughters. Whatever my *Daily Record* wage was for that day ... it wasn't enough.

Tony was a natural choice as cameraman. He had been an 'embedded' photographer during the invasion of Iraq and sent home some award-winning pictures. I'd be beside a man with serious Gulf experience. And I think he was looking forward to returning to the desert to see how things had changed.

RAF Brize Norton is surprisingly like any civilian airport. It has a departure lounge, destination boards, check-in desks and luggage carousels. The only thing that was missing was a bar!

I would be lying if I said the prospect of no booze for a week hadn't crossed my mind. As I packed my bags, there was the temptation to hide a few miniatures of Bacardi in amongst the shampoo and toothpaste.

But I can proudly say I resisted. If the soldiers could go without – so should I. And being caught with any 'contra-band' might jeopardise the whole operation. Imagine the disgrace of being sent home to headlines in the *Sun* newspaper saying '*Record* Man in Gulf Booze Shame'?

The Ministry of Defence had chartered civilian jets for many Gulf troop movements. Climbing on board the Boeing 757, I could have been going to Majorca – except holiday flights don't carry 350 men in desert camouflage uniforms.

First stop was Cyprus, I assume to drop people off or pick up some more, then fly on to Basra. The stewardesses got a bit of ribbing from the lads as they handed out soft drinks. Ten minutes into the mission I was sipping a can of Coke and missing my Bacardi already!

Cyprus was nothing more than a fag break. Off the plane, light up, back on plane. Then off we went again. I managed to grab a window seat for this leg – I was anxious to see what Iraq looked like from the sky. War veterans Major Gene and Tony took a nap.

The window plan quickly fell apart. We were flying east and daylight was disappearing with every minute – soon there was nothing to look at but darkness. I tried to sleep, anticipating getting a look at the lights of Basra as we approached.

But that was knocked on the head as well. Fifteen minutes from landing, we were all ordered to pull down our window blinds.

'Can I keep mine up?' I whispered to the Major.

'Only if you want a ground-to-air missile through it,' he replied. 'The less the ground can see of the plane, the better.' Bob's blind got rammed down pronto!

We disembarked to an arrivals hall that looked as if a bomb had hit it. Then it occurred to me that a bomb HAD hit it – probably lots of bombs in fact.

As we waited for our bags, I spotted a glass exit door and thought I'd nip out for a long awaited smoke. With so much ordnance about, lighting up was banned indoors. As I fumbled for the packet, I heard a 'pop', then a short burst of pops.

Wait a minute. That's GUNFIRE for f**k's sake! I took two quick drags and scuttled back inside.

'I can hear … er … a bit of shooting going on out there,' I said to the Major, trying to sound calm.

'Oh, you'll hear lots of that over the next week,' he smiled. I decided it was time to reacquaint myself with the body armour and helmet that I'd been issued at Brize Norton.

At most airports, you arrive to a welcoming courier who is happy to tell you all about your resort, hotel or planned excursions. At Basra, a big sergeant does the job slightly differently.

He asks you to fill in a form stating your blood group … and the details of your next of kin.

Then it's off to watch a short video that gives you tips on how to avoid being shot, stabbed, kidnapped, blown up, infected, infested, bitten, stung or poisoned.

Tony wasn't showing much interest in the presentation. 'Seen it already …' he shrugged. OK, smart-arse!

All the paperwork complete, we left to where an armoured car was waiting outside. The gunfire was still echoing in the distance and I glanced at the sky looking for bullets whizzing overhead.

'They're miles away …' the Major re-assured me.

We were off to Camp Chindit at a place called Az Zebayr where the Scots Guards 'A' Company had set up base in an old prison. Saddam had used this place for years to keep his enemies in – now his enemies were using it, to keep his friends out!

Aside of the Santa stuff, the Scots Guards wanted to use my visit to highlight the 'hearts and minds' job they were doing at Az Zebayr. As well as peacekeepers, they were also helping to train the Iraqi police force of the future.

I was greeted by Colour Sergeant Gordon Surgeon, an old pal of Ginger George back in Aviemore, where this whole adventure began.

'George said I was to look after you,' he smiled.

'In that case, get the Guinness out and send the birds in.'

'Sorry, no booze and no girls – but we do a lovely tea and biscuits.'

He introduced Tony and me to a few of the lads who had stayed up to greet us. It was now 3.45am and we were both pretty shattered. Gordon showed us to our bunks in a former prison cell – with an ominous-looking steel hook sticking out the ceiling.

'And the toilets are there,' he said, pointing his finger.

I turned around and couldn't see anything.

'No –THERE,' he said again, and I realised he was pointing through the bars of the tiny window. The lavvies were at least a hundred yards away – and it was about seven degrees below outside. I'd already decided I would rather piss in my tin hat than brave going out there.

'Breakfast is at 7.00am.'

'What time does it finish?' I asked, thinking I might need more than the three hours' sleep that was on offer.

'At 7.45,' he answered. I was rapidly going off my Iraqi adventure.

'This is all Gaff's fault. I'm going to kick the wee ginger Hibee's baws when I see him.'

I spent two days with Gordon and his 'A' Company lads. They were a great bunch and I got some good material.

They even invited Tony and me out on patrol with them. We had been briefed that the local kids has wised up to the fact that body armour only protected us from the waist up. Their idea of fun was to stick a rusty knife, fork or nail in your arse – and run away. Yeah, very f*****g funny, I thought.

'It's alright, big man, I'll cover your rear,' giggled Tony.

We toured the town on foot for two hours – probably the longest two hours of my life. I was shit-scared, big time. If somebody had jabbed my bum with a knife – God knows what might have happened next!

Our next base was back in Basra, where 'C' Company was stationed at a place called Camp Cherokee. Conditions were a lot better, with proper showers and toilets. Tony and I went on a dawn raid of some bombed out flats, looking for hidden guns or explosives. The local children begged us for chocolate or sweets – and it was hard not to give in, even though it was frowned upon. Several children had already died, running out in front of cars in the hope they would stop and offer them treats.

Most of the younger kids had no shoes and it struck me that, a thousand feet beneath their muddy little footprints, was enough oil to clothe and feed the whole country. What a f****g mess this country was in.

We then spent a day and night with the 'Recce' Company lads who were stationed at the former Basra airport building, which Saddam turned into a luxury hotel. The luxury was now long gone and the swimming pool was now a sea of green slime with the odd dead dog rotting on the surface.

The 'Recce' lads took us to the Iraq–Iran border and it was an amazing trip. The desert was littered with the rusting hulks of burned-out tanks and other military vehicles. It was bizarre to think that thousands of Iraqis and Iranians had died fighting over these miles of arid wasteland.

The 'Recce' lads had one more thing going for them – an officers' mess. And even better, an old fridge with some tins of cold beer! As I write this sentence, I can still taste it on the back of my sand-coated throat. Sheer heaven!

But the next day was to be a big day. Santa's 'sleigh' had been delayed twice already, but now we learned that our boxes had finally arrived in Basra. It was also a day nearer to going home and I was now looking forward to Guinness, curries, meeting the lads in the Copy Cat – and other home comforts! The excitement of my Iraq trip was starting to wear a bit thin.

I felt sorry for the lads who were looking after me so well. Some faced at least another five months of this. I had been there five days and it was beginning to show. As Tony summed up after an evening of me moaning, 'Shields, you can be a right grumpy bastard!'

The next day WAS a big one – but thanks to Saddam, not Santa.

My mobile rang and it was the office saying that some US news channels had been reporting the capture of Saddam himself. We had heard nothing. I decided to check it out at the Commanding Officer's office – but the sudden noise around me confirmed it was true.

Guns were going off all over Basra and Camp Cherokee was instantly buzzing. It was true – and there was a rush to the TV room to see footage of Saddam being paraded by his American captors.

By now, anyone who had a weapon in Basra was firing it skywards, the air crackled with gunfire. No one knew if this was Saddam's enemies celebrating – or his supporters protesting – but it made some f*****g noise!

The order went out to put on our armoured clothing and helmets which was unprecedented in a fortress barracks like Camp Cherokee. Tony, Major Gene and I ran back to our tent to get our kit on.

'They're not shooting at us, but bullets from the sky can still be dangerous,' said the Major as we jogged.

'I suppose they could give you a nasty bruise ...' I replied.

He looked at me in shock. 'Bob, I've seen a falling bullet go through a car roof, the driver's seat, the car floor and leave a hole in the road ....' Bob ran a bit faster after that!

My mobile rang again and this time it was the happy lads from the Copy Cat bar in Glasgow who had obviously been following events on TV as well.

'Hey, well done, big man! Two armies couldn't flush out Saddam in six months – and you do it in less than a week! Hey! Hey!' The boys were obviously pished again!

Then there was a silence ... and the voice of Billy the manager suddenly sounded a bit more serious.

'Is ... that ... gunfire I can hear?'

'Yes,' I replied, 'the locals are going a bit mental over here. Bullets everywhere ...'

Then I heard Billy addressing the rest of the pub – 'Hey guys, Big Boaby's under fire! I can hear the bullets!'

There were shouts in the background – 'The bastards!' and 'They cannae shoot the Big Shields fella!'

Billy came back on the line, 'Keep the heid doon, big man, and call us back later!'

I couldn't stop laughing ... or wishing I was there with them to share the fun.

If the Allies had been trying to relieve Basra of its weapons, the next few hours proved they had failed miserably. The gunfire went on into the night and included a bullet which landed outside the CO's office and bounced in the door! Tony managed to get a picture of the CO holding it – and I filed a piece about Iraq's reaction to the capture.

That night, I lay in bed staring at the ceiling. If a car couldn't stop a falling bullet – my canvas tent had no f****g chance! I decided to sleep on my side after that, just to reduce the target area. It's great what goes through your mind when it's raining bullets and you haven't had a drink for five days!

We woke up on Christmas Day. Of course, it wasn't really, but Father Christmas was coming and that made it almost official.

I'm sure Major Jim Cruickshank of 'C' Company has done some strange missions in his time but 'Operation Santa' will hopefully be one he remembers with fondness.

He and a team of lads drove us out to Basra airport to pick up the boxes but, after visiting half a dozen offices, no one could tell him where they were. Basra airport covered fifty acres, with just about every one of them filled with packing cases, boxes and cartons.

Tony and I began to fear the worst. Perhaps we'd have to use the dozen or so 'emergency' boxes we'd stashed in our bags. But Major Jim wasn't for giving up. He fanned out his team and we searched for over an hour.

Then, at last, tucked behind a billion bottles of water and several hundred Land Rover tyres, we found a whole a pallet of our boxes.

As they loaded them up, I climbed into my red suit and stuck on the white beard. And that armoured vest of course!

We drove back to Basra with the whole truck singing 'Santa Claus is coming to town'.

While most of the troops had been acting 'cool' about this whole Santa thing, they were secretly quite excited. I had leaked the news that one of the boxes contained a free holiday for two – and word had spread quickly. They crowded around the truck like kids.

'Can we open them now?' one asked.

'Well, it won't make much of a photo if you don't,' said Tony.

What was in the boxes? Well, what WASN'T in them.

Chocolates and sweets, socks and scarves, CDs and a few lads' mags, deodorant and shaving gear, chewing gum and macaroon bars. Plus gallons of Irn-Bru.

A 'C' Company lad called Scott Madden came over and told me 'You have to be stuck out here to appreciate how much this means to us. At this time of year, you think Christmas is for everybody else except you.'

Scott, you made my f****g day!

I later passed around a book for the boys to write messages that would appear in the Christmas Eve issue of the *Daily Record*. They were all so shy at first … but then they poured out their hearts.

'To my darling wife …', 'To my beautiful Lorna …', 'To the son I can't wait to hold …' It was all moving stuff – and I've since donated the book of messages to the Battalion for their museum.

Mission accomplished. It was time to go home.

A few months later, the Scottish Press Awards were held at a top Edinburgh hotel. My 'Send the Jocks a Box' campaign wasn't even worthy of a nomination. I suppose the judges would just see another *Daily Record* 'Our Bob' feature – with me looking like a diddy in a Santa suit.

Fair enough.

But I'm fairly proud of what I achieved from a Sunday afternoon pint.

And the real prize is that, to this day, someone will approach me on the street or in a pub and say, 'It's Willie, from "C" Company … you made my Christmas, big man.'

It's the thought that counts.

9

The Road to Rio:
and a Camel in Marrakech
Gives Me the Hump!

In early 1998, the whole of Scotland seemed to have a spring in its step. Six months ago, we had qualified for the World Cup finals in France.

In December 1997, I was in Paris where FIFA had very kindly paired us with Brazil in the opening match, then Norway in Bordeaux and Morocco in St Etienne.

The *Daily Record* had already sent me around all three cities to prepare a Tartan Army guide for travelling foot soldiers. It had been a great trip and I couldn't wait to get back there in June.

So, it must have been around March when the boss summoned me to his lair.

When his secretary calls you and says, 'Can you pop in and see the editor?', she isn't asking you a question.

Your first thought is usually, 'Oh shit, what have I done?' Your second thought is, 'Oh, shit, what have I not done?' And with my office being only a few strides from his, there was never any time for a third thought.

I walked in and the boss was having coffee with a smiling couple, both dressed for business.

He introduced them as executives from a public relations firm whose clients included the car-manufacturing giant, Vauxhall.

'Bob, they want to talk to you about Norway, Morocco, and Brazil,' he began.

'Yes, I'm looking forward to the games,' I enthused. 'But if I get another call from a long-lost pal looking for a Brazil ticket, I think I'll ...'

'No, Bob, not the games,' the editor interrupted, 'the countries. We're thinking of sending you to Norway, Brazil and Morocco.'

'Sponsored by Vauxhall,' added the nice man in the suit.

You could have knocked me down with an Arctic snow flake, a camel hair or a Copacabana beach girl's thong. It's not every day you are told you're going to visit three different continents – and one of the most exciting cities on the planet.

It was all to do with a marketing campaign by Vauxhall which included a contest to win World Cup tickets. But somebody high up in the car-making firm was a Scot, an avid *Record* reader and someone who liked my ... well ... let's call it 'laid-back' style of writing.

I was to write a fun feature about each country that would tie in with each of Scotland's games. And running alongside each feature would be a Vauxhall sponsored contest to win tickets.

The PR people were delighted that Vauxhall was going to get a good editorial 'show'. The boss was delighted that he would be able to offer his readers some very precious World Cup tickets.

And me? I was grinning like I'd just been told I'd won the lottery during a tour of the Guinness brewery.

People often comment that I seem to have one of the best jobs in the world – jetting around the planet doing unusual things and meeting interesting people. And they're right!

'How do you get a job like that?' they would ask.

I often wish I had the time to tell them about making tea as a seventeen-year-old junior reporter at the *Ayrshire Post*, taking late buses home from boring evening council meetings in Maybole or typing out thousands of winners' names at Ayr Flower Show.

At the *Glasgow Evening Times*, I was on the 7.15am train from Ayr to Glasgow every morning – well, most mornings – to work as a sub-editor for seven years.

When I arrived at the *Daily Record*, I was doing night duties and Sunday shifts. I had probably been a hands-on journalist for two decades before my name ever appeared at the top of a column.

How did I get a job like that? Well, the correct answer would be working my balls off for twenty years! But who really cares … and why should they?

All I can say is that most of my globe-trotting experiences came through ideas I came up with myself.

But if one 'job' was ever delivered to me on a plate – it was this one.

Even then, it's not that simple. My three-continent tour would have to be carefully planned – you don't walk off a plane and straight into a feature story worthy of publication in Scotland's biggest-selling paper.

Contacts had to be established, story ideas set up in advance. I called or faxed British embassies and consulates in all three countries, praying for a friendly Scot who would tell me some titbit that might make an interesting and unusual feature – with a tartan slant.

And there were all the logistical problems like flights and hotels.

I discovered through the British Embassy in Rio that I would require a Brazilian work permit.

I could take the chance and pretend I was a tourist. But the photographer travelling with me would have cases full of professional – and expensive – equipment.

A couple of nights in a South American jail, getting our gear confiscated, being flown home in disgrace and no story to show for a couple of thousand of Vauxhall's pounds wasn't good business.

I flew to London and spent a day at the Brazilian Embassy getting the correct visas for us both.

But finally, the grand plan was in place. And it was a belter! I didn't have a calculator big enough to work out the mileage!

Though Vauxhall's people were picking up a large slice of the tab, there was still a budget to be adhered to. And our travel people advised us that return journeys were always cheaper than one-way trips.

Scotland – Norway – Morocco – Brazil – Scotland would have been nice. But at around £8000 a head, it was a non-starter.

Our 'tour' was Glasgow – Amsterdam – Oslo – Amsterdam – Glasgow – London – Frankfurt – Casablanca – Frankfurt – London – Amsterdam – Rio – São Paulo – Amsterdam – London – Glasgow.

We booked two hotel nights in both Oslo and Casablanca and three nights in Rio – well, it's Rio for f**k's sake! – and off we went.

The photographer on the trip was a wonderful man called Ian Torrance, a *Daily Record* legend and serial award-winner. He'd been on more overseas jobs than I'd had chicken bhoonas. And, hey, that's a lot of bhoonas. I was working with a real pro.

The Oslo leg was … to be honest … hardly an auspicious start. Nothing seemed to gel and our contacts' stories weren't as promising as they sounded by telephone.

We met a lovely Scottish/Norwegian couple whose allegiances would be torn in two when their national teams clashed in Bordeaux. But it was no better than local paper material.

An Oslo evening class teaching bagpipes didn't make any better copy. But we did our best and left with enough material to maybe make the bones of a decent feature.

This was the only 'leg' where we actually hit home base in Scotland. It was bizarre waving Ian off in Glasgow Airport at 7.00pm – knowing I'd be seeing him ten hours later at check-in for our London flight. When I got back to my flat, it was hardly worth emptying the luggage.

'Of all the gin joints in all the towns in all the world …' starts Humphrey Bogart's line from the famous *Casablanca* movie.

As we boarded our flight to Morocco, the 'gin joint' part was preying on my mind: i.e. – did Morocco have ANY friggin' gin joints? Or any 'joints' at all?

World-traveller Ian tried to convince me that, just because Morocco had lots of sand, it wasn't quite Saudi Arabia. But I trousered some of Lutfhansa's miniatures of Bacardi just in case.

After the Glasgow–Frankfurt–Casablanca flights, then a bite of dinner, Ian decided he was going to bed. We had a busy day ahead of us.

But not El Bob. I'd read in an airline magazine about 'Rick's Cafe' at the Hyatt Regency Hotel. Of course, the movie was filmed in Los Angeles and the famous gin joint never actually existed.

But why let the facts get in the way of a good story? I wanted to boast to my pals that I'd been to Rick's in

Casablanca. Even more important, I wanted a beer. So it was on with the kilt – and off in a taxi.

At the Hyatt, Rick's is just off the polished marble foyer, a plush cocktail lounge with giant posters of 'Bogey' and the *Casablanca* movie showing nonstop on giant video screens.

With cold beers costing £6 a pop – only a millionaire could booze long enough for 'Bogey' to deliver his famous closing line – 'Louis, I think this is the beginning of a beautiful friendship.'

The barman was intrigued by the kilt and pretty soon we were talking football in general – and Scotland v Morocco in particular. Like most locals, he followed the French leagues and was a great admirer of John Collins, now manager of Hibs, who at that time played with Monaco.

'Collins – he is best Scottish player, yes?' he asked.

'No,' I told him, 'Collins will be substitute. We have eleven better players than Collins.'

'Aiiieeeee!' he wailed – and darted off to tell the baggage boy about Morocco's impending World Cup doom.

When he returned, he wanted to know who really WAS our best player. I motioned him to come closer, then whispered the name in his ear.

'Allah McCoist ...'

'Aiieeeee!' he wailed again and ran off into the kitchens, never to be seen again.

His replacement was a management-looking guy with suit, shirt and tie. After giving me and my kilt a good eye-balling, he struck up conversation.

'Tonight, here, it is New Year ...' he said.

Ya dancer, I thought. Hogmanay and it was barely June.

'Yes, maybe New Year,' he added.

The word 'maybe' threw me a little.

'Maybe New Year?' I asked.

'Maybe not New Year,' he grinned.

Who does this guy think he is, Kenny Dalglish? Is it mibees aye it's New Year or mibbees naw?

Then he explained that, in Islam, New Year comes with a new moon. And only the holy men can decide if a moon is new or just a wee bit second-hand.

'So, when will they decide?' I asked.

'Tonight, when they can see the moon,' he replied, not unreasonably.

I had visions of this happening back in Scotland. The whole country, sitting around with carry-outs and bowls of cheesy nibbles, waiting on somebody to tell them it was officially Hogmanay.

Perhaps it was the possibility of a New Year that was gradually drawing more and more locals – and a few Westerners – through the hotel's revolving doors. But most of them slipped off down a flight of stairs.

'What's in there?' I asked Kenny Dalglish.

'Nightclub,' he smiled.

Well, what was a boy to do? I downed my beer, gave Kenny a few dirhams as a tip and followed the crowd downstairs for a bit of Casablanca boogie.

At the curtained doorway, a giant of a man in shirt and bowtie suddenly hoved into view. Doing a fine impression of a traffic policeman – he shoved the palm of his hand out in front of me.

'No!' he growled.

'Eh?'

'Nightclub not for you. You wear dress,' he added, pointing to my kilt.

Well, nobody calls my kilt a 'dress' – especially not on Hogmanay, for goodness' sake. Mind you, this boy was built like the side of a mosque. And he was probably 'tooled up' Moroccan style – with one of those curly-wurly knife things under his jacket.

I headed back upstairs where Kenny Dalglish was still working – at least I knew he could speak reasonable English. But when I explained my problem, he simply shrugged his shoulders. I don't think he fancied tangling with the curly-wurly knifeman either.

So I demanded to see the manager. 'Le directeur de l'hôtel, maintenant!' I insisted.

Kenny poured me a beer and asked me to wait. Sure enough, a smartly-dressed man in an immaculate silk suit appeared with another manager tagging along.

He introduced himself in perfect English and asked what the problem was.

I introduced myself as Jim Farry, president of the Scottish Football Association. Well ... I did have a couple of bevvies in me!

I told him I was in Morocco on football business prior to our World Cup meeting.

'Le Coup de Monde,' he nodded. The World Cup was obviously a big buzz word in this soccer-crazy country.

I explained I was wearing the national dress of my country and was greatly offended that his staff had refused me admission because of it.

I asked how he would feel if a Moroccan came to Scotland and was treated in a similar fashion. And I then delivered my final salvo, 'This will be in my report to FIFA!'

The boss man was clearly shaken. He shouted something in what sounded like Arabic and a few more suited staff appeared from nowhere.

Then they disappeared down the stairs where I could just make out some more Arabic being shouted. When things quietened down, he invited me to follow him downstairs.

The men in suits had all gone ... but so had Mr Curly-Wurly. Poor guy – he was probably gone forever.

The manager escorted me straight through the curtains and up to the bar. 'Champagne for Monsieur Farreeee!' he said, clicking his fingers. And a silver ice bucket with a bottle of Moët et Chandon appeared at my side.

Ya beauty! Being Jim Farry was getting to be fun.

The manager hovered beside me for a few minutes, nodding to passing waiters with the obvious message that I was his personal guest.

Finally, he put his hand out to shake mine and motioned that he wanted a quiet word in my ear. He gave my kilt a final once-over then whispered, 'Mr Farree ... with respect, I ask you not to dance'.

So that was it. Me and the kilt were welcome – but bopping the disco floor, showing my knees to the locals, was too much to bear.

I didn't really care. I'd made my point and got some free bubbles in the process. So I downed another few glasses and slipped off to get a taxi outside that revolving door.

The moon looked huge in the starry North African sky. On a couple of streets, locals were partying and letting off firecrackers. The holy men had obviously given Ne'erday the go ahead.

The next morning, I went down for breakfast where Ian was already tucking into some eggs and toast.

'Morning!' he chirped.

'Happy New Year!' I replied.

'Eh?'

'It's a long story ...' I yawned.

But we had a long day ahead for me to tell him everything.

One of our first stops was the British Consulate where the man in charge was forty-year-old Charles Mochan from Dumbarton. A fitba' man himself, he gave us some good background on Moroccan football and the local club, Raja, which had just become African Cup holders.

He also had great local knowledge and told us we must visit the amazing Hassam II Mosque.

Built for the King's sixtieth birthday in 1993, it took 6000 Moroccan craftsmen five years to complete. Its 600-foot minaret was, and perhaps still is, the tallest in the world.

Holding up to 25,000 worshippers, it comes complete with heated floor, retractable roof and a laser beam that points the way to Mecca.

But the one thing Charles couldn't help us with was … a camel.

Ian reckoned a camel with a tartan scarf around its long neck would be a great picture.

However, looking for a camel in downtown Casablanca was a bit like coming to Scotland and looking for a Highland deer in Sauchiehall Street.

Charlie recommended we take a trip south to Marrakech. And he put us in touch with a local driver who spoke good English. We finished our business in Casablanca and booked our driver for the next morning.

Marrakech. And we still had Rio to come the day after. I felt like nipping down to the mosque and thanking Allah personally. It was turning out to be one of the best trips ever.

The next day we jumped into our limo – an old, battered but very clean Mercedes. I was singing the old Crosby, Stills and Nash song, 'Marrakech Express' as we drove out the city.

It was a dusty, two-hour journey – a long, thirsty way to go for a major disappointment. Marrakech is Arabic for 'Don't linger here', and whoever named the place was spot on.

Bus loads of noisy German, Italian and American tourists swamped the place. And the locals were mostly skilled in one ancient craft – parting you from your dirhams.

The beautifully dressed Berber water sellers no longer sold cupfuls of life-saving water from their goatskin bags. They made their living by getting their pictures taken by Chuck and Beth from San Diego.

The camel drivers don't do any driving and the snake charmers could use a term at charm school. They were no more than beggars. Girls offering you henna tattoos followed you around until you paid them to go away.

When we finally found a bar, you had to push a dozen cannabis and hash sellers out the way just to get a swally. And it was warm, tinned piss.

We spotted a camel driver and bartered our way to a photograph. The locals aren't diddies – they can tell a dinky Canon Sure Shot owner from a professional lensman like Ian. And the price went up accordingly.

My particular camel looked older than Marrakech itself – and the city had been a trading post since 3000BC! It had carried so many tourists, its hump was worn down to a lump.

It was also stinking. As 'Bogey' might have said, out of all the camels in all the deserts in all the world, I had to find one that farted from both ends. At the same time.

And when we finally tied a scarf to its neck, the old f****r started to chew it!

Then Ian decided a shot of kilted Bob aboard the camel would make a good picture. It's one of the few times I wished I wasn't a true Scotsman!

This camel didn't just have fleas – its fleas had fleas. Sir David Attenborough could have made a whole series about the life on this manky beast. And I was about to park my bare botty on it!

There were probably diseases on this camel that Western medicine hadn't even got names for yet.

Of course, a kilted Scotsman on a tartan-decked camel in

the middle of Marrakech isn't exactly an everyday event.

Suddenly, there were a dozen and then a hundred more cameras than Ian's – all pointing at me.

I didn't mind posing for a few seconds, in the best interests of international goodwill and promoting Scotland, of course.

But I suddenly noticed the driver had let go of the reins and had wandered off to flash his begging bowl at his new, record-breaking audience. Ian was busy keeping both eyes on his camera gear and was helpless to intervene.

I was shitting myself that the camel would panic and do a runner – next stop the Sahara with Bob on the back!

I tried to restrain my language and be as diplomatic as I could. But the words that came out were 'Hey, ya greedy old bastard, get me off this f*****g camel!'

But he wasn't listening. The longer I stayed up there, the more dirham notes landed in his begging bowl. I was the camel-driving equivalent of a tartan lotto ticket.

When I finally did get off, the old git had enough money to build a Hassam II Mosque of his own.

It was back to the car and straight back to Casablanca and the hotel. I couldn't wait to get water and soap on my dangly bits.

The next day, we had to fly to Rio and I didn't fancy twenty hours on a plane with an honours degree in etymology running around my undercarriage!

After dinner and a visit to a local souk, we called it a day. And what a memorable day it had been.

I scratched myself to sleep thinking of the girls waiting for me on Copacabana beach.

Roll on Rio!

10

The Road to Rio:
My Date with Ronnie Biggs
... in a Gay Bar!

I'M usually pretty jammy when it comes to nabbing a window seat on a flight. If all else fails, telling the check-in girl that I'm claustrophobic and might have a panic attack if trapped between two passengers usually does the trick.

But on the haul from Frankfurt to Rio, all my attempts had failed – and I was mightily pissed off.

We'd be landing in late afternoon sunshine and I wanted to see the sweep of Copacabana beach, the mighty Sugar Loaf Mountain and the majestic statue of Christ the Redeemer at Corcovado from the sky.

But it was not to be. I spent the fourteen hours wedged between snoring photographer Ian and a sweaty Brazilian with a nose hair problem. This guy had a pony tail sprouting from each nostril, and I swear they grew another half inch during the flight.

However, it wasn't totally wasted time. I swotted up on the city that awaited me – for example, Rio de Janeiro means 'River of January' and the huge bay it now stands on was discovered on New Year's Day, 1502.

Back then, it was a shallow beach where ships could send boats ashore for fresh water and maybe fresh fruit. Today, it is a city of ten millions souls – twice the population of Scotland.

One of those ten million was a mad taxi driver called Zeca. He picked us up at the airport and whisked us to our hotel, giving us a running commentary all the way about local points of interest.

At the Holiday Inn, he volunteered to be our driver/guide for the next few days and gave us his mobile number.

Ian and I stashed our gear in our rooms and went down to the hotel bar for a bite to eat. After a few beers, we were both yawning and stretching – we had been awake for almost twenty-four hours.

'Think I'll call it a day,' said Ian.

'Eh?'

'Bedtime. We have a big day tomorrow ...' he continued.

'But Ian ... it's Rio ... it's Saturday night. How many f****g Saturday nights will you ever spend in Rio?'

Ian conceded the point but said he was too tired for a night on the town. I told him I was determined to go out and was quite happy to do so myself.

'But where will you go, Bob?' he said with genuine concern.

'Copacabana.'

'How will you find it?'

I went into my shirt pocket, pulled out the business card Zeca had left us and waved it in front of Ian.

'OK then ... but I'll come along with you, just for a nightcap of course.'

Nightcap my arse! The old professional in Ian had stirred. I was unashamedly going to look at the birds and check out the booze.

But Ian would be looking at the light, the scale of the beach, backgrounds and anything else that might help him take a better picture. The lure of a quick peek at one of the most famous beaches in the world was too much for him.

The grinning Zeca arrived and off we went. It was only a ten minute journey and Zeca explained the Copacabana tourist ground rules, most of which were common sense.

Expensive-looking watches, jewellery and cameras were an easy target for thieves – especially at night time.

'Will I be OK with my cameras in daylight?' asked Ian.

'Oh yes ... if Zeca is there to watch out for you!' cackled our driver. Old Zeca didn't miss a trick.

He also warned us not to flash wads of money about – and not to buy street souvenirs.

He told of a scam about a vendor selling little samba drums. On a given signal, a souvenir packed with cocaine would be sold to an innocent tourist.

Around the corner, two policemen would pounce and 'discover' the hidden drugs. The poor tourist was then taken away to be charged – being told during the journey that he or she faced up to fifteen years in a Brazilian pokey.

But just outside the police station, the car would stop and the officers would make their 'generous' offer. Give them all your valuables, then empty all your credit cards at a cash machine. In return, you would be released without charge. Zeca said it was an offer nobody refused.

And within minutes, the cocaine-filled souvenir would be back with the vendor, who would be given his cut before setting up their next victim.

Zeca dropped us off and I got my first glimpse of Copacabana. In the fading sunlight, people were mostly packing up to go home though a few groups were playing 'foot-volley' – a version of beach volleyball but played using your feet.

The skills on display were amazing and the players seemed to be barely in their teens.

I tried to imagine this sport at home on Ayr beach. If the wind didn't blow the ball halfway to Arran, the players would be up to their ankles in jobbies and condoms!

Ian and I walked along the front and sipped another beer at a beach kiosk. After a few more yawns, he decided he wanted to head back to the hotel and bed. Despite my bleary eyes, I was having none of it. Bob was out to play.

Ian hopped in a cab and I sauntered off in search of another swally, finally stumbling on a bar that had live football on TV. A team called Botafogo were playing a team called Vasco da Gama and it seemed to be a bit of a local derby. I recognised the Botafogo colours from a little footballer that dangled from Zeca's rear-view mirror in his cab. If Vasco da Gama won, he'd be good for a 'wind up' when we met him tomorrow.

It was then I felt a tap on my shoulder … and turned to face one of the most striking women I'd ever seen. Dark skinned, long dark hair and a voluptuous body that was falling out of a skimpy silk two-piece.

If she had slinked into any bar in Glasgow, she would have dislocated every neck within a hundred yard radius. In this Rio beach bar, no one's eyes moved from the match.

She produced a cigarette and gestured for a light. The best I could fumblingly offer was a book of Holiday Inn matches I'd swiped at the hotel.

'Where are you from?' she purred, in very good English.
'Scotland,' I replied.
'Ah, Scotland, it is very beautiful, yes?' she asked.

By sheer coincidence, the words 'very beautiful' just happened to be spinning around the Shields napper at that very moment.

'I have always wanted to visit Scotland ...' she continued, sliding her body onto the bar stool next to mine. As she sat, her silk top fell open, leaving nothing to the imagination. And a slit in her skirt appeared, right to the top of her thigh.

At this point, feel free to re-arrange the words 'eyes', 'head' and 'popped out'.

If the lady's movement was slick, the barman's was even slicker. The moment her perfectly formed rear-end touched the bar stool, he was over to ask if I wanted to buy my new friend a drink.

I had been down this road before. The girl asks for an expensive cocktail but gets a fresh orange, decked out with fancy fruit, instead. And splits the difference with the barman later.

To my surprise, she asked if I would buy her a beer. Well, what's a man to do in Rio on a Saturday night?

We made polite conversation. Her name was Lina, she was from a town I'd never heard of and had come to Rio to study to be a nurse. She liked football and her favourite player was Romário. And Brazil were going to win the World Cup.

At this point, I confess to thinking that if I had Lina at home, I wouldn't even watch the World Cup.

But after fifteen minutes of chat and having drained most of her beer, it was time for the lovely Lina to get to the point. Again, it was done with real Brazilian style.

'You know, I do massage to help pay for my studies,' she smiled.

'Really?'

'Yes, at my flat, it is just around the corner ... would you like me to massage you?'

I'd be lying if I said I wasn't sorely tempted. My hormones were saying 'yes' – but my head was listening to

Zeca's warnings about all the things that can befall the unwary on the mean streets of Rio.

I had visions of Lina's extra-large boyfriend waiting around the corner – ready to massage me with a baseball bat.

'Maybe another time,' I finally stuttered.

'I could give you a very special massage … anything you want,' was her final, pleading sales pitch.

'Sorry, Lina, I don't think so,' was the best rejection I could offer.

Lina pecked me on the forehead, said something in Spanish or Portuguese to the barman, and walked out.

I ordered another beer. Lina had been such a beautiful distraction, I hadn't noticed Botafogo had taken a one goal lead. Zeca would be a very happy boy.

The barman poured the beer and gave me a shrug of his shoulders. 'Nice girl, Lina. Fifty dollars USA for one hour – but maybe you get her for thirty …'

I looked outside and Lina was still there, talking to a blonde. I turned away and heard the sound of heels on the wooden floor, then felt another tap on my shoulder. It was Lina's friend – maybe she believed in the old addage that gentlemen prefer blondes.

Again, she was a real stunner. And again, we went through the same routine. She asked for a light, asked me where I came from, then sat down.

'You buy the lady a drink?' asked the barman.

'Sorry – maybe another time.'

The blonde stood up, straightened her dress and calmly walked out to where Lina was waiting.

I decided it was time to drink up. Having turned down a dusky brunette and a stunning blonde – I didn't even want to guess what they'd send in next!

I grabbed a cab where the driver was listening to the football results – 'Botafogo 2, Vasco da Gama 0'. I wondered if they had fixed odds in Brazil – and if Zeca had a bet on.

It was now at least thirty hours since I'd seen a bed. I body-swerved the Holiday Inn bar and went straight to my room.

A balmy Saturday night, in the razzle-dazzle city of Rio … and I was tucked under the covers before midnight. Shields – you're a wimp!

* * *

Despite Rio's obvious distractions, we were here with a forthcoming World Cup in mind. And football crazy Zeca was to prove invaluable over the next two days.

The next morning, he took us to Corcovado, the hill overlooking Rio that is home to its most famous landmark – the statue of Christ the Redeemer.

It's an impressive sight and has a small museum that explains how over 1000 tons of stone was carried up the hill, then hoisted up the statue to complete it. As well as a tribute to Christ, it's a tribute to man's ingenuity.

The view from the top is equally stunning. I have gazed over New York from the top of the Empire State building and seen the sprawl of Hong Kong from The Peak. But nothing matches the vista from Christ's feet at the top of Corcovado.

Sugar Loaf Mountain, the city and the beaches are laid on in front of you. Behind you is the famous 200,000 seat Maracana Stadium.

And off to the left in the distance is a giant sprawl that looks like a jumble of crazy paving.

'Dona Marta – the favela …' said Zeca.

I had read about Rio's infamous 'favelas' – the shanty towns that are home to millions. In places like Los Angeles or Hong Kong, it's the rich that look down on the rest of the city from their posh hillside palaces in Beverly Hills or Victoria Peak.

But in Rio, it's the poor who cling to the mountainsides like leeches, sucking every last ounce of survival from their favela footholds.

Rio's wealthy would never build there. During tropical storms, torrents of water flood down the mountainside, bringing with it a wall of mud that overwhelms anything in its path.

Zeca told us that, two years before, eighty people had died when twelve inches of rain fell in forty-eight hours.

But every day is a risk for the favela folk. These people are non-citizens – no rights, no benefits, no medical care. The few schools are run by local charities – with the blessing of the local gang lords. Not even Rio's police dare set foot in a favela.

Yet even in the poorest areas, where every square foot of land is worth a knife fight for, there is always room for a football pitch.

It won't have nets or goalposts, it probably won't even have a blade of grass. But for the children of the favela, even the tiniest piece of waste ground is big enough to dream on.

The little boys who live here don't want to win *Pop Idol* or *The X Factor*. They never see themselves as millionaire traders in the locally grown coffee, sugar or even cocaine.

They want to play football. They want to play for Flamengo, Vasco da Gama or Zeca's beloved Botafogo. But most of all, they want to climb the mountain behind them and play at the Maracana. They want to play for Brazil.

Players like Zico, Romário and Ronaldo rose from the favelas and there is no shortage of kids waiting to follow in their golden footsteps.

As Zeca explained, with no little emotion in his voice, 'To play for Brazil is to be a king. And to wear the No. 10 shirt at the Maracana is to be a God.'

Not even Zeca's presence would guarantee us safe passage in a favela. But the British Embassy in Rio had told us of a Scots teacher and charity worker, Evlyn Marshall, who worked in a school at the edge of the teeming Dona Marta. She might get us limited access for Ian to take some pictures of children playing football which would be more than useful for our World Cup feature.

Sure enough, Evlyn came up trumps and as I stood nervously watching the doorways and shadows, Ian got some great pictures.

Zeca followed up our football theme by suggesting we go to the beach where a local radio station was sponsoring a mini-tournament for kids.

You didn't need to hold me back. These favelas were scaring the shit out me – and Copacabana meant beer and girls!

It was a joy to sit with a cold one and watch the 'beautiful game' in its infancy. Somewhere, out there in the sand and sunshine, was the next Ronaldo or Roberto Carlos.

And further up the beach were the beautiful girls. Ian suggested a picture of me striding past the bikini-clad tottie in my kilt would be fun.

And fun it was. Nobody told me the girls sunbathed in an area popular with gay men. I don't know what these thong-wearers were shouting at me – maybe they wanted to know if I wore one under my kilt.

But the first gay who wanted to take a look for himself was going to get a boot in the coconuts!

Why Rio should have such a large gay population intrigued me – especially when the city boasts the world's most beautiful women.

But even more intriguing was a snippet from our friends at the British Embassy that a Scot owned a Rio pub called 'The Loch Ness'.

'Yes, I know of it,' said Zeca. 'It's a gay bar,' he grinned.

Gay or straight, a Scot running a boozer in Rio could be a great story. So off we went – although I did change out of my kilt to avoid any … er … embarrassment.

The Loch Ness was a fine looking pub, and behind the bar was a strapping big Scotsman called Billy Biggar. And beside him was his beautiful Brazilian wife. If Billy was gay … I was Carlos Alberto.

Billy grew up on Clydeside watching a boat getting built at the foot of his garden. It was the mighty *QE2*.

Billy promised himself that, one day, he'd sail on the giant liner that burgeoned daily in front of his young eyes. And he was no dreamer.

His promise came true when he landed a job as a chef for *QE2* owners Cunard, and he sailed around the world several times.

'I always fancied having my own business one day,' he told me.

'I had been to most of the world's great cities with the *QE2*, but there was just something special about Rio. So I decided to cash in my savings and make a new life here.'

It was hard not to smile at the rest of his tale.

'I worked hard and built up a good pub business, we were very popular with ex-pats and obviously any Scots.

'But then a gay bar opened along the street. Then, a gay restaurant across the road … then another gay bar. Suddenly, the street had the reputation as a gay haunt – and I was running a "straight" bar, said Billy.

'My "straight" customers wouldn't come to a gay area – and the gays wouldn't come to a "straight" bar. So something had to give – and we went gay.'

Billy was generous with his beers, good company and knew a lot about local football. Best of all, he was Tartan Army crazy. So Ian took some pictures and we talked football for ages.

Then he came out with the kind of remark that would seem fairly insignificant to him – but stopped a journalist like me in mid gulp.

'Ronnie Biggs drinks here.'

'Eh?'

'Aye, you just missed him. Most of the gays come in after work, so Ronnie comes in early, has a few drinks, then he leaves before they turn up. He's one of my best mates now.'

From a feature point of view, Billy's life and his gay boozer was a great story. But Ronnie Biggs was the icing on the pink cake!

'Will he be in tomorrow?' I asked.

'No reason why not. I'll call him later and check out that he's happy to talk to you,' said Billy. 'He often speaks to journalists. They bung him a few quid and he gets some beer money. I think it's his only income these days.'

Billy and I met up later for some more beers and football talk – but he confirmed that Ronnie was up for a chat and would be in around 4.00pm the next day.

The rest of the night is still a bit of a haze to this day. But one of the clubs we visited made headlines a few years ago when some Manchester United directors got into a bit of bother with some local girls. I wonder if one of them was called Lina?

But I woke up the next morning with a stinking hangover. Only the thought of meeting the legendary Great Train Robber made me feel a bit better.

Rio's traffic that afternoon was a nightmare and even Zeca's unique knowledge of its side streets wasn't going to get us there on time.

When we finally screeched to a halt outside The Loch Ness, I threw open the car door without looking and almost knocked over a white-haired gentleman with a walking stick.

'I'm sorry, are you alright?' I asked as he straightened himself up.

The old man smiled, 'Ere … you must be that Jock I'm supposed to meet. I never mistake a Scots accent'.

So, on the steps of a Scots-owned gay bar in Rio, I finally shook hands with Ronald Arthur Biggs.

Ronnie looked frail and Billy had forewarned me that he was recovering from a stroke. He looked older than his sixty-eight years although his sixty-ninth birthday was just days away.

His most memorable birthday however would have to be his thirty-fourth.

It was on his birthday in 1963 that he and others halted and robbed a Royal Mail train from Glasgow to London.

His 'present' to himself was £140,000 – worth about £2.5 million today. By his thirty-seventh birthday it had all gone.

Photographer Ian and I had already had a long discussion about Ronnie's past. Although he had 'celebrity' status, he was still a convicted criminal, and a train driver had died following injuries received during the infamous theft.

'How the f**k do you work a Great Train Robber into a World Cup feature about Scotland?' I had asked myself.

The obvious answer was to ask Ronnie some football questions – and hope for the best. And the best is what we got.

Ronnie revealed he was a football fanatic and was disappointed that his stroke would cost him a summer job as a World Cup commentator for a Brazilian TV station.

'I don't suppose you'll be supporting Scotland?' I joked.

'Well, funnily enough, I'm a bit of a Hibs supporter,' he replied.

Biggsy? A Hibee? You couldn't make this up ...

'Well, one of the first games I ever saw as a kid was a friendly between Arsenal and Hibernian at Highbury. I guess something stuck with me because I always look at the papers to see how they're getting on. Does that make me a Hibs fan?' he asked.

Too f*****g right it does, Biggsy boy!

'Well, that's our Scottish connection,' I said to Ian.

'Hey, if you want Jock stories, I'm your man,' laughed Ronnie. And for the next half hour, he held us spellbound.

Ronnie revealed that it was a Scot who helped him escape from Wandsworth Prison all those years ago.

'The plan was to go over the wall and onto the roof of a furniture van. But we need someone to start a fight and distract the 'screws'.

'There was a young lad from Glasgow whom I thought I could trust with details of the escape. I offered him five hundred quid if he would help me out.

'But this Jock said he didn't want my money, he would do it for the honour of helping Biggsy escape. Imagine a Jock turning down money, eh?' he grinned.

'The poor bastard got twelve months onto his stretch. To this day, I don't know who he was and I've never ever thanked him.'

Ronnie went on to tell how another anonymous Scot helped him escape capture in Australia.

'I had plastic surgery, a new identity and was settled in Australia. Then one day, the phone rings and it's a geezer with a Scots accent. He tells me the police are on to me and I've only got a couple of hours to get away. We packed our bags and legged it. The police were there about an hour later. I still don't know the name of the Jock who tipped me off.'

But Biggsy will never forget the name of the third 'Jock' to feature large in his life story, John Miller.

He was the ex-Scots Guardsman who twice tried to kidnap Biggs and bring him back to Britain.

'He was a nasty piece of work,' said Biggs.

Billy put on a tartan 'Jimmy' hat we'd brought from Scotland and poured Ronnie a malt. Ronnie asked if he could try the hat on … and Ian was there with a camera to capture the moment.

I could almost hear the call we'd be getting from the *Daily Record* office later.

'Well, what have you got today?'

'Not much … just an exclusive interview with Ronnie Biggs and a picture of him in a "Jimmy" hat … '

Ronnie took the hat off and held it in his palm for a second.

'You know, when we opened the mail bags after the robbery, most of it was cash. But one package had a little tartan bonnet in it. I remember thinking it was probably a nice present for someone … a present that would probably never arrive.

'When I see tartan hats, I sometimes think of that little bonnet …'

As Ian checked his film, I shouted on Billy to get another round of drinks up. The day had been a great success and I knew, even then, it would be a special day in my career as a journalist.

'Ronnie, would you like a large … ?'

But there was no one there. The walking stick beside the bar was gone as well.

Ronnie Biggs had escaped again.

11

And the Winner Is ...
My Night at the Oscars

THE very first Academy Awards ceremony was held in the Blossom Room of the Hollywood Roosevelt Hotel in Los Angeles in 1929. It wasn't a great success. The winners had already been announced in the early editions of the *Los Angeles Times* and guests could buy a paper on the way in!

A seat at the dinner cost $10.

It would be almost another seventy years before I got to the Hollywood Roosevelt Hotel. And ten bucks wasn't enough to tip the valet parking attendant.

It was 1996 and the movie business was gripped by a midget Australian playing a giant Scotsman. His face painted like a Tartan Army footsoldier and with a dreadful Scots accent, this American funded movie, filmed mostly in Ireland, was an instant hit.

Braveheart was the talk of the steamie and was tipped to win a clutch of Oscars. Despite its international background, Scotland claimed the film as its own and Mel Gibson became a national hero.

The editor of Scotland's biggest selling newspaper wisely decided that we should be represented at this most prestigious of award ceremonies. And even more wisely, decided to send little old me!

With the Oscars in the bag, I chanced my luck by suggesting I might use the trans-Atlantic journey to also cover the Mike Tyson v Frank Bruno heavyweight title fight in Las Vegas the week before. And he agreed to that as well. This editor was surely the wisest man in Christendom!

I'll leave the story of Las Vegas for another day. Our arrival co-incided with the dreadful events at Dunblane and, literally overnight, the reporting of two guys beating the shit out of each other for a couple of million dollars wasn't so appealing.

At one point, I suggested photographer Bill Fleming and I return to Scotland. But the boss said there was so much sadness back home that any glitz and glam from the Oscars might bring some welcome light relief.

Such was the on-off nature of the trip, Bill and I arrived at LAX airport without so much as a hotel reservation. But we did have a hired car. As I'm a non-driver, it was down to poor Bill to bravely steer our Buick onto a highway that was four times as wide as the runway we had just landed on.

I turned the radio on, rolled down the window, lit up a Marlboro and pulled on my shades. I could get used to this LA lifestyle.

Things weren't going quite as well for Bill. We were on an eight-lane-wide Interstate and Bill had already upset horn-honking drivers travelling behind us in at least seven of them!

'I don't know where the f**k we're going!' he pleaded.

'Hollywood,' I told him.

'And where's that?'

'Over there,' I said, pointing, 'where that big wooden sign says "Hollywood"!'

God bless Bill, he got us there no problem. We parked up near Gruman's Chinese Theatre and the famous 'Walk of Fame' which I assumed was about as central Hollywood as you could get.

We grabbed some beers at a bar on Hollywood and Vine and came up with a game plan. Our accommodation budget was $150 dollars a night – and if we found anything cheaper than that, the difference would go straight into the communal swally fund.

But Bill was carrying a lot of expensive equipment and was rightly concerned that the low budget rooms would also mean low budget security. We went through a list of hotels, I kept voting 'swally' and Bill kept insisting on security.

So we strolled down a few blocks to see what was available and came across the Hollywood Roosevelt.

Price-wise, it was more or less on the money, seemed to be well policed by security staff – and they had rooms. We shook hands on our choice of accommodation.

But it was only after we brought the car around that we realised that parking charges – plus tips – would add another fifty bucks a day to the bill. Suddenly, the communal swally fund was in a negative equity situation! Bill thought this was hilarious.

That evening, I suddenly took a craving for an Indian curry. It had been a long time since my last one and I was sure a multi-ethnic metropolis like LA would have a wee Indian restaurant somewhere. Bill was up for the same.

I asked the hotel information desk if they knew of any Indian eating places.

'Well, sir, I'm sure you'll get something of that nature at a place called Buffalo Bill's Chuck Wagon which is …'

I felt obliged to interrupt him.

'No, we don't mean North American Indian, we mean … er … like Indian Indian.'

'Indian Indian, sir?'

'Yes, India – you know, the pointy bit between Africa and China …'

Thankfully, one his assistants overheard our conversation and came to our rescue.

'I think I know of a place on Hollywood Boulevard, it's called the Star of Bengal, I could look it up for you, sir?'

The Star of Bengal! Now we're cooking! He got us an address and off we went.

The Star of Bengal was in a little mall and was everything you could hope for. The flock wallpaper, the sitar music, red velour seating and pictures of the Taj Mahal everywhere. Plus all my old favourites were on the menu.

It was near the end of the night and, from our window seat, Bill and I watched a man stagger his way toward us, a shopping bag in one hand. He fell in the door, slurred a few words, picked up his order and staggered back out again.

'Look at that, Bill – it's closing time, he's pished out his brains, he's got a carry-out in one hand and an Indian take-away in the other. Fantastic!'

'Aye – it's wee moments like this that remind you of home,' he said wistfully. We laughed our way back to the Roosevelt.

The next day, poor Bill had to brave the highway to hell again. We needed to go downtown to sort out our press accreditation for the Oscars ceremony itself. I was already fearing the worst: official accreditation applications had closed about a month ago. Our only option was to play up the fact we'd flown 6000 miles for the ceremony, tell a lie that Mel Gibson had personally invited us … and generally act like a couple of complete diddies. The diddy part would not take an Oscar-winning performance. The Scottish bumpkins were out of their depth.

The press office girl did her best to be helpful – but rules were rules. The Academy worked a press accreditation system that was tighter than a submarine's window. I had been to World Cup finals and Olympic Games – but the Academy was in a league of its own.

Gold Badge holders got the freedom of the city. They could go anywhere at anytime – these were the guys who patrolled the famous 'red carpet' with microphones and cameras. Silver Badge holders got access to a press area where the stars were interviewed before or after the ceremony. Bronze Badge holders got to a press zone where they could watch the Silver Badge holders on a live TV feed. And there were Blue and Green Badge holders even lower down the food chain than that.

Bill and I got issued with Black Badge status.

I politely asked what this press pass entitled us to.

'Well, you guys can go pretty much where you want. However, the badges expire on Sunday at 6.00pm.'

'But ... er ... the ceremony is on Monday.'

'That's correct, sir. I'm sorry, but it's the best we can do.'

F*****g marvellous! We had accreditation that expired before the ceremony had even begun!

I made a call to Fiona Phillips, the GMTV presenter, who at that time was their Hollywood showbiz correspondent. We had arranged an interview with her the next morning and I asked if there was anything else we could do. She did her best to be helpful but explained that the Hollywood press scene was pretty strict.

Fiona gave us a good interview – including the news that she was moving back to the UK to share 'the sofa' with Eamon Holmes. It was a new story and I was delighted she shared it with us. She also told us about the British Academy's pre-Oscar party at a hotel the next day.

The venue was a very posh beachside hotel called Shutters on the Shore. Fiona said that all the Oscar Brits would be there, but wasn't quite sure who was in town. However, she reckoned than Emma Thompson and Sir Anthony Hopkins would be two of the better known names attending.

So far, all we had gathered story and picture wise was the centre of a doughnut. We had visited the Oscar ceremony building, the Dorothy Chandler Pavilion, to talk to some of the nutters who were already camping out on the pavement to get the best view of the stars coming down the famous red carpet.

Our Black Badge also got us access to photograph the carpet fitters – no, I'm not f*****g kidding! – and the official Oscar florist.

The British Academy party was our first chance to get near some real movie stars – and give us something to put in Monday's paper.

We left the Roosevelt early as we doubted our navigational skills. Mind you, the fact that the hotel was on the beach, and the beach just happened to be the Pacific Ocean, was a bit of a clue.

So far, every time we had asked directions at the hotel, the first instruction was always 'hang a left at Fairfax' – Fairfax being a famous Hollywood main street.

It had now become a bit of a standing joke. It seemed impossible to go anywhere in LA without 'hanging a left at Fairfax'. One night, after few bevvies of course, we began asking the bar staff bogus directions, just to hear the Fairfax reference.

After breakfast on Sunday morning, we both went to the information desk to ask directions to Shutters on the Shore. We could hardly contain ourselves.

'Well, sir, you hang a left on Fairfax ...'

That was it. Bill and I started giggling so much that we ended doubled up on the floor. The poor guy behind the desk must have though we were a couple of imbeciles.

To this day, whenever Bill and I meet, one of us will get 'hang a left at Fairfax' into the conversation somehow.

We arrived at Shutters on the Shore ridiculously early – the shutters were definitely still down. But a few metal barriers for crowd control were already in place, so we knew we had the right venue and entrance.

We went for a stroll on the boardwalk where the first joggers and roller-bladers were doing their thing.

I sat on a bench and began taking off my socks and shoes.

'What you doing?' asked Bill.

'Going in to the water.'

'What for … ?'

'It's the Pacific, Bill. I've never set foot in the Pacific before …'

'Shields, you're f*****g mad,' said Bill.

But off I went, trousers rolled up to the knees, for my first ever Pacific paddle. I went in up to my ankles and gazed out to sea, wondering what lay beyond the horizon.

The next thing I know, Bill is there beside me, with his trousers rolled up to his knees as well. The shoreline joggers, tanned, fit and wearing UCLA vests, stared in disbelief as Bill and I splashed about like it was Saltcoats at Glasgow Fair.

We had time for a coffee before heading back to Shutters, where a small posse of press had already gathered. Bill got his cameras from the car and we strolled into the press pack, all neatly in line behind the barrier.

'Hey, you, what the hell do you think you're doing?' yelled a man with a camera around his neck.

Bill looked around, just in case this guy was targeting someone else. But he wasn't.

'You ... you can't stand there! That place has been taken!' he shouted again, this time with more than a hint of aggressiveness. The press posse suddenly stopped chattering ... and looked at Bill.

Now Bill isn't exactly Arnold Schwarzenegger, but he's not a man to take liberties with – and certainly not when he's in work mode.

'Listen pal ... I didn't fly 6000 miles for you to tell me where I can and cannot f****g stand! Have you got a f****g problem wi' that?'

Nice one, Bill. His forthright reply caught the guy a little off guard.

'But ... your name's not on the list,' he insisted.

'List? Stick your list up your arse!' Bill countered.

Another snapper stepped in to calm things down.

'I guess you guys aren't from around here.'

'We're from Scotland, over for *Braveheart* at the Oscars,' I told him.

He pointed to a piece of paper, with some names scribbled on it, tied to the metal barrier with some string.

'Well, over here we use a list. You put your name down when you arrive and that keeps your place if you wanna go for a coffee or something.'

'We ... don't do lists in Scotland,' said Bill, which was meant more as an explanation than an apology.

Suddenly, everyone became a bit friendlier. It turned out that most of the photographers there were LA freelancers – and this was their bread and butter.

When they realised that Bill wouldn't be sending to local agencies and threatening their livelihoods, all was well again. But Bill still never moved from his spot.

Our new friend explained how things should work out.

The guests all arrive by car and most will happily pose for a picture. Then they go inside for cocktails while the press go to another suite.

Some of the 'stars' will look into the press room to give interviews. If not, you can hand a member of staff your card that will be passed onto the person you want to interview.

Sure enough, Emma Thompson turned up – and so did Sir Anthony, though they didn't hang about for pictures. But to be honest, most of the other faces we simply didn't recognise. The man we really wanted to show up, Sean Connery, was nowhere to be seen.

It was much the same inside the press suite. I doubted if any of these 'stars' were really Brits at all.

We were getting a little frustrated: I had no quotes and Bill had hardly fired off a frame.

Then Bill gave me a nudge and pointed to a man standing on his own with a coffee. It was Mickey Dolenz.

'Fancy a chat with Mickey – at least people have heard of him,' said Bill.

'Bill – who gives a monkey's about Mickey Dolenz?'

Another fit of the giggles set in. We weren't getting much work done – but Bill and I were having a fun day.

It was time to go for broke. We went to the hallway outside the cocktail room and I handed a business card to a waiter. 'Sir Anthony is expecting me,' I lied.

We stood around for about ten minutes, and just when we were about to give up, a door opened and out strolled old Hannibal Lecter himself.

'My dear fellow, you've come all the way from Scotland, how lovely to see you here,' he said.

I was quite taken aback – he was talking to me as if I was a long-lost friend.

He also has the most amazing blue eyes … Hannibal Lecter's eyes.

However, my interview with Sir Anthony was suddenly going back to front. He was asking ME all the questions, about our journey over and our hotel etc.

Thankfully, Bill had got the cameras out as was clicking away.

When I mentioned the Tyson v Bruno fight, Sir Anthony confessed he hadn't seen it and asked for a blow by blow account.

'Well, there weren't too many blows – Bruno stood motionless like a tree while Tyson chopped him down,' was my fight summary.

'Motionless … like a tree … very descriptive,' he smiled.

I was just about to ask my first Oscars-related question when someone, his agent I suppose, grabbed his elbow.

'Anthony, you must come and meet …'

Hannibal offered his hand and gave mine a firm shake. 'Lovely to have spoken to you, enjoy your stay in Los Angeles …' And off he went!

As interviews go, it wasn't an interview at all. If anything, he had interviewed me.

But with pictures taken at the venue, some of the look-a-like stars at the Walk of Fame and now Sir Anthony, we had enough to make a decent pre-Oscar spread. It was time to head for Fairfax – and the Roosevelt Hotel – to get writing.

The following day was Oscar day … the same day our Black Badges became even more worthless pieces of plastic than they already were.

A lunchtime swally in the Hard Rock Café at Rodeo Drive – which we kidded ourselves was a star-spotting opportunity – didn't make our situation any better.

We had flown across an ocean and a continent to cover the Oscars … and we wouldn't be getting anywhere near it.

Back at the Roosevelt, we changed into our dinner suits. The strict Academy rules state that all press, including even

TV cameramen, must wear formal attire. At least we looked the part. Downstairs in the lobby, everyone was wearing the same. The hotel was probably full of visiting journalists – but most of the bastards probably had press badges!

For luck, we asked the information desk directions to the Dorothy Chandler Pavilion.

'Sir, first you got to hang a left on Fairfax ...'

You couldn't make this place up.

Bill risked the highway to hell once more, but I think he was getting used to it by now. All the radio channels were either coming live from the venue, or playing famous movie themes.

The ceremony was a few hours away, but the crowds were already huge. Bill looked for a vantage point, an office or a balcony, but most were filled with people having their Oscar night parties.

We checked out the entire block surrounding the Dorothy Chandler Pavilion, it was, as the Americans would say, 'in lockdown'. Bill and I were in the shit, deep shit.

I then noticed that, while the red carpet and entrance area were filled with police and security staff, the area at the bottom of the street wasn't.

It's human nature that if you expect someone to be somewhere – like a man in dinner suit where lots of men in dinner suits should be – suspicions aren't immediately aroused.

There were lots of photographers flashing away at men in dinner suits. And I had the very photographer ready to flash like crazy – just for me! Bill thought I was crazy as well – but he couldn't wait to give it a try.

We hopped the security fence and Bill set his camera to flash. And off we went towards the entrance.

Bill was hamming it up big style – 'Just one more picture please ...could you turn your head this way, sir?'

Me? I thought it was great. Posing for a flashing camera at the Oscars – this would be as near as I'd ever get to becoming a movie star.

By now we had passed two security guards who must have assumed I was some celeb on my way to the entrance.

'Sir, one of you beside the Oscar, please?' said Bill. I was right at the doorway guarded by those two giant Oscar statues you see on TV. Bill let loose another couple of flashes.

They say 'he who hesitates is lost' – and that's exactly what happened to me. I should have gone through the entrance – just walked right in like I was Tom Hanks.

Maybe someone inside would have asked for an invitation or some ID – and caught us out. But we never got the chance to find out.

For a moment, we stood like a couple of diddies, like rabbits caught in a headlight. A security man came over and asked Bill for his accreditation. Then he asked for mine.

I managed to produce the Black Badge we'd been given earlier. Maybe he wouldn't realise it was a worthless piece of plastic shit. But our moment had gone.

'I'm sorry, sir, but this pass is not valid for this area. Can I please ask you to leave?'

The game was a bogey. Bill and I trudged down the way we had came.

On the way up, I was being photographed like a movie star … on the way down, I was another bum without a ticket to the party.

'What now?' asked Bill.

'We go back to the hotel and watch the Oscars?' I suggested.

Bill agreed – there was nothing else we could do. At least we would see who had won what, and get any quotes that

Mel Gibson might give to TV. Then we would come out again and try our luck at the after-show parties.

The hotel was having its own Oscar party on a big screen in the cocktail bar. We joined in the fun – even if we were the only two plonkers in dinner suits.

Mel did better than anyone had hoped for. *Braveheart* won five Oscars – it would be THE big news tomorrow – and Mel Gibson was the only star in Tinseltown.

Fiona Phillips had tipped us off that Mel would probably head for a party at a famous restaurant called Chasens. It had been booked by the studio who made *Braveheart* and Mel would be obliged to turn up and give homage to his paymasters – and their wives of course.

There was a huge press pack, all waiting for Mel. There were floodlights and helicopters flying overhead. It was Hollywood mayhem.

Bill and I squeezed into a gap next to a female TV reporter and her crew. When she turned around – it was BBC girl Jackie Bird. And she was more than a little taken aback.

Maybe Jackie thought she was the only Scottish-based journalist in town and could see her 'exclusive' going down the pan. But she wasn't a happy bunny.

'You can't stand there,' she huffed. Now where had we heard that line before?

'Come on, Jackie, the BBC don't have any more rights than we have,' I told her. Jackie, her microphone tied with a little tartan ribbon, then decided to ignore us.

I had a little tartan surprise of my own – a scarf hidden in my dinner suit pocket. Bill thought it was a great idea. All we needed now was Mel …

We waited over an hour, but the word among the press posse was that Braveheart was on his way. Limo after limo pulled up – Michael Douglas in one of them with a bevvy of beauties – but no sign of the man.

Then, a screech of tyres and some yelling and screaming. Limo doors flew open and Mel Gibson almost fell out. It was safe to assume that Chasens wouldn't be serving him his first swally of the night.

He had an Oscar in each hand and waved them to the crowd – they cheered like crazy. Then he made his way past the line of photographers, stopping for a few seconds if he recognised them.

As he approached, I got my scarf out and leaned over the barrier.

'A little gift from the people of Scotland. Congratulations!' I shouted.

Mel had both his hands full – with glistening Oscar statues.

'Thanks, you'll need to put it on for me,' he said.

I leaned over and put the scarf around his neck. I was trying to turn to one side to give Bill an angle with his camera.

'Say "hi" to Scotland for me,' said Mel, then he disappeared down the line.

I was more than chuffed. On this night, Mel Gibson was the most sought after man in the world. And we had him in a picture exclusive.

'I can't believe we got him,' I grinned at Bill.

'Well, don't say that until we've seen what's in the camera,' he cautioned. Remember, these were the days before digital.

'Bill, tell me you've got the f*****g picture!'

'There was a bit of pushing … but I think we might be OK.'

'MIGHT be OK?'

We jumped in the Buick and headed for hell's highway and the inevitable Fairfax. It was now after 1.00am and we hadn't eaten since lunchtime.

Bill decided to pull over at a burger bar.

In our excitement, we hadn't given any thought to where we might be.

Bill stayed with the cameras and I strolled into the burger joint with a fistful of dollars in my hand.

Whoah! Haud on a minute!

I was the only white face in the whole place, if not the whole street. And I was certainly the only white guy in a dinner suit in the whole neighbourhood!

I couldn't just turn around and walk out. So I walked up to the counter and ordered two burgers, two fries and two Cokes. The guy took my order and disappeared into the kitchen – seconds later, four black faces peered out at me.

I looked around and there were four more serious looking dudes all staring at me. I spotted a large glass ashtray sitting on the counter. Any trouble, the first guy got the ashtray and I was out the door.

The burgers appeared, I told the guy to keep the change and strolled back out again. Then I ran like f**k to the car.

The door was locked, I couldn't believe it. I hammered the window and there was Bill, head back and eyes closed, having a post-Oscar nap.

'Bill, wake up! Get me f*****g out of here!.'

Back at the hotel, Bill went to his room to start work on developing the film. I made a stop in the cocktail bar – the burger joint had freaked me out.

Bill's phone would be unplugged to connect his wiring machine, so the only way of checking was to dash up and down to his room.

I must have made six trips, with my constant interruptions making Bill even more exasperated.

But on the seventh trip, I rang Bill's door and he greeted me with a huge smile.

'Pictures are fine ... Mel, the scarf and you ... they're not perfect but they'll do ...'

Within hours, they were plastered all over the front page of the *Daily Record*.

And within hours, Bill and I were just plastered!

12

Tonight's the Night ...
Rod Stewart Might Buy Me a
Drink!

WHEN your name is Rod Stewart, you need journalists hanging around your door like General Custer needed more Indians. But sometimes, what we press people call 'door-stepping' is the last chance of getting the quotes or picture you want.

In June 1996, everyone wanted rocker Rod. Scotland were about to play England in a European Championship double-header and the Tartan Army's most famous fan headed the tartan media's 'most wanted' list.

All the usual channels, via his agent or his record company, had failed.

I was ready to leave for London and Wembley when the boss suggested I stop by Rod's house and 'chance it'.

Maybe it's an old-fashioned Scottish thing, but I never like to go to someone's house empty-handed.

I was once asked to interview entertainer Jimmy Logan, and the only time that suited him was 9.00am on a Sunday morning. I wondered what I would like someone to bring me at that time of the day.

So I pitched up at his door with six fresh morning rolls and a packet of bacon. You would have thought I'd brought him the Crown jewels!

So what should I take Rod? The obvious would be tartan bunnets or scarves – but Rod probably had cupboards full of them.

Knowing that Rod is a doting dad, I decided to appeal to his fatherly instincts.

I checked press cuttings to discover the ages of his youngest ones – they told me daughter Renee was aged four and little Liam only two.

And, on my way to the airport, I stopped at a sports shop to buy little Scotland kits in that age group.

Thankfully, London-based snapper John Dempsie knew the location of Rod's house in Epping, which was just as well. It's a country pile well off the beaten track. He met me at Heathrow and off we went.

Rod's place had an electronic gate with a call-button. So I pushed 'speak' and announced myself.

'It's Bob Shields from the *Daily Record* here. Any chance of a quick word about tomorrow's game with Rod? Oh, and can you tell him I've brought a little present from Scotland for Renee and Liam?'

I knew it was a bit of a ruse. And you can bet a wily old fox like Rod knew it was a ruse as well. But hey, what was there to lose? And Rod has always been a good sport when it comes to Scotland.

'Wait there,' said a voice at the other end. So we waited … and waited.

Meanwhile, a few cars started arriving and after a quick word on the call-button, were allowed straight past the electronic gates. Eagle-eyed John spotted one of them was Arsenal and England striker Ian Wright.

'Looks like Rod's playing football,' said John.

And still we waited. If the voice had said 'Go away!' we'd be in the boozer by now. But 'Wait there' gave us hope enough to continue guard duty for a little longer.

We were rewarded with the sight of a shapely blonde striding towards us. It was Rod's wife, Rachel. She was wearing a white blouse, jodhpurs and a pair of riding boots. She looked sensational.

'Bob?'

'That's me,' I blushed.

'Rod's got a game on – but he says he'll see you in the village later for a pint.'

'That's great, thank him very much – and tell him I've a little something for the wee ones.'

'Shall I take it …'

'No, er, it might make a photo for us later,' I stammered.

Gazing at the gorgeous Rachel, I almost fell for it. But I knew that if I'd given her our packages, they'd be inside and we'd still be outside.

Rachel strode back towards the house. She probably thought our eyes followed the sway of her jodhpurs all the way down the drive. And she'd be absolutely right!

John and I climbed back in his car.

'Right – the village pub!' I said gleefully.

'What village?' asked John.

'Er … the village, you know. THE village.'

'This place is full of f****g villages,' said John.

'Well, it's the one where Rod goes for a pint …'

'You should have asked,' chided John.

'Sorry, I wasn't thinking straight.'

We decided our best bet was the nearest village, and sure enough, it had a quaint village boozer.

I decided it might be an idea to check with the barman if this was, indeed, Mr Stewart's regular watering hole.

'Yeah, he'll be along, mate. This is usually a football night for him,' he said, drying a glass.

'You down for the match?'

'Yeah.'

'Well, we're gonna hump you Jocks tomorrow. Three – nil. No danger, mate.'

'No chance. Colin Hendry will have Alan Shearer in his back pocket.'

'Yeah, mate, and while he's watching Shearer, Gazza will be getting a hat-trick.'

It was all good fun –and a few locals joined the big soccer debate. Rod had good taste in pubs.

We watched the car park for Rod and he eventually appeared, in an open-topped sports car.

Heads turned when he arrived, but it was obvious the locals were used to seeing him drop in. And Rod seemed more than comfortable.

'Bob, how you doin', mate?' He smiled. 'What you havin'?'

Now, this was a moment I had pondered over. An old mate of mine, journalist Russell Kyle, used to be very pally with Rod. And he told me that in all the years he'd known him, Rod had never bought a drink.

'Rod buying ME a drink – wait until Kyle hears this,' I was smirking.

'Eh, a pint of Caffrey's for me, please, Rod.'

'Two Caffs,' Rod ordered.

The barman poured the beers and served them up, 'That's £3.80, thanks'.

Rod grabbed the pints, turned to one of his party and said, 'Sort that out, mate.' And walked away.

Hey, Russell, maybe you've got something there!

We had our beers outside and presented him with the little Scotland kits. Rod was a total gent, posing up for a few pix and talking excitedly about the big game.

Exclusive story and pictures in the bag. Job done.

I've met Rod several times since. The most recent was a Hampden match where he gave me a lift from the Rogano restaurant in Glasgow to the game.

His wee lad had grown up a lot since I bought him that Scotland kit, and Rod did the introductions.

'Liam, this is the famous Bob Shields,' he said. I winced ... but was really quite chuffed. Rod was born to flatter blondes. Even this one!

A few years before that, Rod and I had shared a Bacardi bevvy in his dressing room.

I was more than happy to get to a tot of rum for it was Baltic outside. Wait a minute ... it WAS the Baltic outside.

I was in Kiel in Germany to present Rod with an official 'Tartan Army' tartan suit. He was also due in Scotland the following week and I'd get a preview of the show he'd be putting on at Glasgow's SECC.

I listened as Rod did his soundcheck and chatted to some of the band and crew. The tour backstage passes featured Rod and Denis Law, and a giant lion rampant was the stage backdrop. Rod wears his love of Scotland well.

On the down side, his agent was a real harridan. Maybe they have to be, but this woman was rude for fun and harder than the ice on the lake outside.

I'd flown to Copenhagen and been stuck in a car for hours ... to give Rod a free suit. You'd have thought I'd come to eviscerate his testicles.

'You have TEN minutes,' she ordered, as we disappeared into his dressing room with the suit.

Rod was giving his voice a good warm-up ... 'Stay with Me' he'd sing until he was happy with the tone or the pitch or whatever the f**k singers do.

'What you havin, Bob?' he asked.

I could see a bottle of Bacardi had already been broached, so I asked for a rum and Coke.

Rod looked for a glass – but eventually settled for what looked like a flower vase someone had forgotten to put the dressing room blooms in. He tipped the rest of the rum in, scooped a handful of ice from a bucket and added a full can of Coke.

Russell Kyle's theory that Rod never buys a drink may or may nor be true. But f**k me, he knows how to pour one!

The suit fitting went fine – Rod loved it. And we chatted about Scotland's on-the-field fortunes.

The old boot of an agent eventually came in to tell us our ten minutes was up.

'F**k off ... we're talking football here!' he shouted. I couldn't have put it more politely myself.

With me was Ian Adie, who designed the 'Tartan Army' tartan and had enjoyed a fling in the charts with his World Cup song, 'Scotland Be Good'.

Rod said his daughter had been playing Ian's CD the night before – and Ian immediately offered Rod a signed version.

'That would be great,' said the world famous rock star ... to the one-hit wonder.

Ian was chuffed. So chuffed, that he talked about 'autographing my CD for Rod Stewart' all night ... and all the way home. And STILL talks about it!

Rod gave another good interview, including his denial of a story in a rival paper that he was buying shares in his beloved Celtic. That's always a journalistic bonus ball.

I watched the show and it was fantastic – but I thought Rod might have kicked one of those signed footballs in my direction. I'd just given him a free suit for f**k's sake!

But he's a great man and a great performer. And whatever you say about his accent or his birthplace, he's a great Scot.

I look forward to him buying me that drink soon!

13

I Reached for the Sky ... then I Reached for the Sick Bag!

IT'S every little boy's dream. And, let's be honest about it, it's every big boy's dream as well. I'd wanted to be a fighter pilot since *Reach for the Sky* when Kenneth More still had two legs.

So one crisp December morning, I finally found myself at RAF Lossiemouth. That same morning, I also found myself at Huntly, Portsoy, Rosehearty, Ballater, Pitlochry, Spean Bridge, Eigg, Skye and Easter Ross.

Travelling by MacBrayne's, this journey would have taken a week. Travelling RAF, it was all over before the pubs had opened!

We've all seen Jaguar jets – those little green darts that flash past so fast, you don't even hear them until the pilot's landed, retired and bought a cottage in Devon.

Getting to sit in one, however, can a be a long process.

I had previously done some Ministry of Defence 'facility' trips – including a memorable trip to the Belize jungle with the Scots Guards.

For local newspapers, it's usually a great chance to feature a local lad having a great time in the army, navy or air force.

But national newspapers look for something with a bit more 'meat' in it.

My Belize feature had a 'warts and all' edge, giving the glamorous and unglamorous sides of army life equal billing.

Somebody at the MoD's press office seemed to like this more 'realistic' approach and further invitations followed, including a tremendous trip to Madrid for a joint exercise with the Spanish Royal Guards.

I think this was my reward for enduring the poisonous snakes and spiders of jungle Belize. It was British Airways Club Class and five-star all the way. The Spanish had laid on enough wine to float King Juan's palace. It was one 'El' of a piss-up!

I recall one night when there was nothing officially planned and an officer asked me if there was anything in particular I wanted to do.

Leicester City were playing Athletico Madrid that evening and I'd read that Athletico's fans were some of the most colourful and passionate in Europe.

'I would mind going to the match,' I said, almost as a joke.

The officer returned minutes later to inform me that transport, a driver and tickets had been arranged. It was a tremendous night and I recall Leicester putting up a fighting display, encouraged every minute by their 'jack-in-the-box' young manager.

'He's one for the future,' I thought. His name was Martin O'Neill.

How I managed to get the invitation to fly in a Jaguar will never be known. These things can burn £10,000 of fuel in an hour and seats in the cockpit don't get handed out as raffle prizes.

But I think there had been some negative press about low flying jets in the Scottish Highlands. I assume the RAF wanted to put their case that low flying was a vital part of pilot training and it was done with sensitivity to populated areas.

Somewhere in the corridors of Whitehall, my name had come up on a list. And I couldn't have been more delighted.

There were all sorts of forms to be filled in. And the press relations guy was more than interested in the state of my health. I got the impression that a heart attack at 250 feet wasn't what they wanted.

It was only later I discovered that they had to be satisfied that I'd survive on a snow-covered peak or in the freezing North Sea in the event that we had to eject in an emergency.

I went over all the relevant medical stuff on the phone to Whitehall and was quite happy until the RAF man threw in a sneaky one.

'I think the weight limit is about fourteen stones – but we don't have to worry about that, do we Bob?'

It's a good job we were talking over the phone – or he would see that I hadn't been that weight since the Battle of Britain.

Fourteen f****g stones! I needed a pint to Guinness to think about this one.

I could confess I was over the limit and get 'grounded'. Or I could try and shed a few pounds in the six weeks or so left to flying day. After four or five pints, the latter option won!

I went home that night and, when my partner wasn't looking, hopped on the bathroom scales. I was clocking in at ten pounds over the limit – but it wasn't as bad as I thought. I could lose that no bother.

If the truth be told, my 'diet plan' didn't begin for another five weeks, In fact, it was the f****g day before we were due to fly!

I had been warned that the pre-flight medical would include a blood test for alcohol. I decided that I wouldn't have a drink during the twenty-four hours before take-off. How very considerate of me!

I travelled by train to Elgin and missed the hotel dining room's opening hours, which was maybe a good thing.

The temptation to go out for a fish supper was almost overwhelming – but I resisted. And surely a pint wouldn't do me any harm? But I resisted that as well.

I awoke the next morning sober, refreshed … and basically shitting myself. The RAF man had advised me to eat something before the flight, so I had a cup of tea and half an omelette for breakfast. For some reason, this made me feel even worse.

At 16 (R) Squadron RAF Lossiemouth, there were more offers of tea and biscuits, which I also declined. I didn't want to fail the weigh-in thanks to a caramel wafer.

First up was the medical – which I was dreading as much as the flying. I was convinced they would find something awful in me somewhere. They tested my urine, heart, lungs, eyes, blood pressure and reflexes.

Unbelievably, I was declared fit to fly. Even more incredibly, no one had produced the dreaded set of scales that would surely prove I was over the limit.

I thought that was about to end when another officer appeared and looked me up and down.

'Mmmm – you're a big lad …' he mused.

'Well, I suppose I am a bit overweight,' I muttered.

'No – I mean "big" as in height … we'll need to check you out.'

It never occurred to me that, at six foot, I might be too tall to fly.

They put me in a straight-backed chair and produced a piece of stick. Then measured the stick against the line of my back and hips to the front of my knee.

They explained that this hip to knee length was critical.

'The stick is the distance from the cockpit seat to the control canopy. If your knee is longer than that, it will be under the canopy. In the event of an emergency and you had to eject, everything below your knee would be left in the plane.'

'F*****g hell,' I muttered.

'Exactly,' said the officer.

Thankfully, I appeared to be within regulation size – or at least I thought I was. When I got to the equipment section, the gents' outfitters of RAF Lossiemouth, Senior Aircraftsman Carl Evans had other ideas.

Jaguar pilots wear five different layers – thermal underwear, woollen suit, rubber suit, flight suits and then assorted safety gear.

As I slipped on layer after layer, I was beginning to take on Billy Bunter proportions. And when it came to the green flight suit, the zip finally hit the fan. It wouldn't budge past my multi-layered gut.

I pulled and twisted, I tried breathing in and tightening what was left of my stomach muscles – but the zip wouldn't move.

'Have you nothing larger?' I asked.

S/A Evans was now getting slightly pissed off.

'Sir, this is the RAF – not Burton's the F*****g Tailors. If you can't get into that – you can't fly.'

My faced reddened at the thought of the shame – too fat to fly. I had been bragging about this flight to the boys in the Copy Cat for months. They'd rip the piss out me big style – 'Did they no have a Hercules you could squeeze into?' they'd laugh.

I ended up on my back while S/A Evans literally stood on my stomach and pulled at the zip. With a final heave – it moved at last. I felt like a pot-bellied pig stuffed into a condom.

But, at last, I was ready to fly.

'Anything you want to do before you go?' I was asked. What I really wanted to do involved taking all five layers off again. So I had a fag instead.

For my pilot, 16 (R) Squadron produced the main man, the Top Gun, the Officer Commanding – Wing Commander Brian Newby. Aged forty-two, he'd logged more hours in Jaguars than I had logged in boozers. Well, almost.

He explained that we'd be doing a flight typical of the squadron's role – turning RAF pilots into RAF Jaguar pilots. It's called an Operational Conversion Unit.

On this sortie, we would be simulating low level attacks on computer generated targets. But not too low level, I hoped.

As I strolled out across the apron, helmet in hand, I had that *Top Gun* moment. I felt a million dollars.

But a million pounds wouldn't even be the deposit on the beast in front of me. Fifty-four feet long, half that from wing tip to wing tip and more horsepower than all the Grand Nationals put together.

An aircraftsman helped me into the cockpit, tightened my helmet and strapped me in. His last job was pulling the safety pin from my ejector seat. I was now sitting on an unexploded bomb.

The Wingco's instruction had been quite clear, 'If I shout "eject, eject, eject"- pull the handle and go. After the third "eject", I won't be here to help you!'

'Roger.'

It was a gentle take-off, not much different from Glasgow–Palma with Direct Holidays. But then he went into a deep sweeping turn, just a few hundred feet over Spey Bay, that threw my breakfast down to my ankles.

'You OK, Bob?' I heard though my earphones.

'Fine,' I lied. I was scared stiff.

We screamed inland past Dufftown to line up our first 'target', a marked buoy off Rosehearty. Brian was giving me a running commentary, but by the time he explained what was in front of us – it was already ten miles behind us.

The screens lit up as he fired our electronic rockets at the target. Brian explained that we had scored a 'hit' – but our missiles had struck two seconds early.

Two seconds? For f**k's sake driver, get a grip up there!

Then he pulled his sharpest turn yet and my gravity suit – 'G-suit' – kicked into action. Turns like this force the blood from your top half to your bottom half – and could lead to blackouts as it drains from your brain.

The pressure suit squeezes your legs to force the blood back up again. It's like having your blood pressure taken – on both legs at the same time.

This manoeuvre made my breakfast move again. Why did I have the f*****g omelette in the first place? I had gone from queasy to feeling very sick indeed.

'You OK?' asked the skipper again.

But I knew that he knew I wasn't. He could obviously hear my gulps and dry wretches in his earphones.

We passed Pitlochry, then Loch Rannoch. We skipped over a rainstorm as Eigg and Rhum loomed ahead. Rhum? The way I was feeling, I'd never have another f*****g rum again!

A fierce right hander and the majestic Cullins of Skye lay ahead, basking in sunlight and shadow.

I was moved … but so was my stomach. I flipped down my oxygen mask and reached for a conveniently placed sick bag.

The rest, as they say, was breakfast.

After that, I didn't feel so bad. I had been fighting being sick so much, I wasn't enjoying myself. But now, the battle lost, I was determined to admire Brian's flying skills as he weaved past mountains and through glens.

For the first half of the flight – I just wanted him to land. For the second half, I wanted to sit in the cockpit all day.

When we finally landed, I almost fell down the steps. My old legs had turned to rubber. Something I hadn't noticed, until I took my helmet off, was that I was drenched in gallons of sweat.

The skipper took his helmet off and shook my hand. He looked as if he'd just played a rubber of bridge in the officer's mess.

Every time I see a fighter jet now, I think of that day.

I look up and wonder if it's a brave young pilot on Operational Conversion Unit duty ... or some poor journalist trying to keep his f****g omelette down!

14

Walter Smith Gave Me My Pre-Match Orders ... 'Bob, Don't Let "Goughie" Get a Kick!'

In the Spring of 1997, I'd barely heard of Kansas City. I remember it used to appear on a burning map at the beginning of the cowboy series *Bonanza*.

When Hoss, Little Joe and all the other Cartwrights were roping steers and shooting baddies, Kansas City was the stepping stone to Oregon, the Santa Fe Trail and the New World.

It was certainly a whole new world for the man I'd flown to Kansas to interview. His name was Richard Gough.

For almost a decade, 'Goughie' had been a colossus at Ibrox for Glasgow Rangers. He had helped them to eight league titles in a row – and a possible ninth championship was looming.

But Richard had also announced at the start of the season that it would be his last with the club. He had signed a deal to join the Kansas City Wizards.

A leg injury had put Richard temporarily on the Ibrox sidelines, and he had sought and received the club's permission to make a brief visit to Kansas, do some pre-season publicity for his new club and attend to some business regarding his future house.

Maurice Johnston, formerly of Ibrox – in fact, formerly of just about every other f*****g club you can think of – was a Kansas player and had been instrumental in persuading his old pal to head west.

I reckoned Gougie and Mo-Jo combined were enough of an attraction to send me Stateside with my notebook for a nosey.

It would also be a chance to snap the Rangers legend wearing his new colours for the first time. That WAS the picture.

But the middle of Missouri is a long way to go for a 'knock-back'.

Before I left, Richard had said he was quite happy to pose up in his new team's kit. But he asked me to clear it with Rangers' manager Walter Smith first.

Gough was still a contracted Rangers player and was very much in Walter's plans for the final surge towards the dream of 'nine in a row'. So I called Ibrox for Walter's approval.

'Bob, I don't care what colour of f*****g jersey he wears, just as long as he's fit to wear a f*****g blue one when he gets back!' said the mild-mannered Ibrox boss. 'And, Bob, make sure those Americans don't try to tempt him into farting around in some daft kick-about. In fact, don't let him near a f*****g ball at all!'

'I'll look after him, no danger,' I replied.

So that was that. Rangers' hopes of equalling Celtic's 'nine a row' record were now down to Fat Bob man-marking one of the legends of the game!

I was looking forward to the trip. I had never been to the Midwest, or wherever the hell Kansas City was, and I'd be working with a photographer called Craig Halkett for the first time.

'Hawkeye' was a sports specialist and had worked with Goughie many times through Rangers and Scotland.

From all reports, he was a good guy to work beside, and it didn't take long to find out we were both on the same wavelength.

After breakfast on our first morning, we strolled out to the steps of the Kansas City Holiday Inn to get our first look at the place in daylight.

It was just after 9.00am and our meeting at Arrowhead Stadium, home to the Wizards and the American footballers the Kansas City Chiefs, wasn't until noon.

Already, a painted sign across the street had caught my attention. It read 'Bar and Saloon – Open 24 Hours'.

'We've a couple of hours to kill, what do you fancy doing?' asked Hawkeye.

'Well, I fancy walking across the street and having us a couple of beers,' I replied. Hawkeye let out a sign of relief.

'Thank f**k for that! I was going to suggest that myself – but I didn't want you to think I had a drink problem!' he laughed.

A few bottles and a cab ride later, we arrived at Arrowhead Stadium. Its capacity is 87,000 – and the Chiefs' average attendance is … 87,000. On a good day, the Wizards can attract gates of 15,000 – a lot less that Goughie was used to entertaining.

The Ranger had already arrived and was in and out of meetings, no doubt getting to know the stadium staff and club executives.

We were warmly welcomed by club officials who seemed very excited to have landed a player of Goughie's stature. And they invited us to come back the next morning for their 'Media Day'.

Mmmmm …'Media Day'. Hawkeye and I immediately didn't like the sound of 'Media Day'. It meant other journalists and photographers sending f**k knows what to f**k knows where.

Walter Smith was right, we would have to keep an eye on our Mr Gough. Especially if we wanted to be the only newspaper to have him wearing his new club jersey.

We finally caught up with Goughie and had a chat about his exciting new future and the wrench of leaving Rangers. To stop the feature being too 'sports section', we also got him talking about his family and how much he hoped they would like their new life in America.

We also briefly met Mo-Jo, who was polite but a little wary of seeing Scottish media on his home turf. Mo-Jo still bore the scars of what his life was like in Scotland after he famously crossed the 'Old Firm' divide.

We also made some attempt to get Goughie into his jersey, so we had the picture 'in the bag' – just in case 'Media Day' brought us unnecessary grief. But the 'locker room' was living up to its name – and the man with the key has pissed off for the day. Imagine being at Ibrox or Celtic Park and unable to get your hands on a team jersey? Goddam Americans!

However, it was a successful day, even though poor Hawkeye only had a few stadium shots to show for it.

In the taxi back to our hotel, we talked 'sah-ker' with the driver.

He told us that the Kansas City Wizards had changed their name from the Kansas City Wiz.

'They had to,' he laughed. 'In this town, a "wiz" is what a man does in the restroom after a few beers!'

Was he taking the piss or what?

After dinner, Hawkeye and I spent the evening playing darts and sipping the local brew at the twenty-four-hour saloon.

We got chatting to a barmaid who told us she was only doing the job to pay for her final year at college. She was obviously a very intelligent girl … well, by American standards anyway.

'Where you guys from?' she asked.

'Scotland.'

'Now where exactly is that? Is that in Europe somewhere?'

'Yes.'

'Well, I have to say, you guys speak VERY good English.'

'Thank you.'

It was another example of what I have found on many visits to the USA – they are very insular and know little about other parts of the world.

Next day was 'Media Day' and we were first at the Arrowhead Stadium. We didn't want any surprises – like another Scottish newspaper pitching up.

But it was all local press, TV and radio, and there weren't too many of them either. If Rangers or Celtic had made a star signing and this was his first visit to his new home, the place would be jumping with journalists.

But these guys seemed unaware of who Richard Gough was or what he had done. They had probably never even heard of Rangers and, on last night's evidence, probably never even heard of Scotland either.

We stood back in slight shock as 'Media Day' unfolded. Not enough media had turned up for the original plan – for the press to play the f*****g first team!

Imagine that back in Scotland. Rangers v the Scottish Press at Ibrox and Nacho Novo is bearing down on goal with only Jim Traynor to beat. Holy shit!

Instead, they organised a penalty shoot-out thing, American style. You were handed the ball in the centre circle and had to run upfield with it and try to beat the goalkeeper.

I watched some of the home journalists have a go – and they were pretty hopeless. But, to be fair, no doubt our guys would be the same in a reverse situation when asked to perform a couple of basic 'plays' at American football.

Finally, I was handed the ball by the referee – who was Goughie. Richard had obviously taken Walter Smith's warning to heart and refused to get involved.

I looked upfield to find the Wizards had changed their goalkeeper ... I'd be up against Maurice Johnston.

I may have put on the pounds and lost a bit of speed – OK, I didn't have any f*****g speed at all – but I reckoned I had enough of the old 'Silky Shields' skills left to beat Mo-Jo.

Most of the other guys had tried a panicky shot the moment the keeper advanced near them. But that wasn't for old 'Silky'.

Oh no. I'd draw Mo-Jo out his net, dink it past his left, run around his right, and tap into the empty goal. Easy.

I trailed the ball towards the goal and Mo-Jo advanced. I was heading straight for him. Just when he'd committed himself, I side footed past him and turned to run around the other side. It was all going to plan.

Then 'whack!' Mo-Jo's boot caught me somewhere above the knee and I went down like a William Hills coupon. The ball was still rolling slowly toward the goal, so I struggled up and chased it ... but it trickled just wide of the post. Bastard!

'For f**k's sake Mo, it's meant to be fun,' said Goughie.

'I know,' grinned Mo-Jo, 'but how often to you get the chance to kick a c**t from the *Daily Record*?'

We all had a good laugh. Mo-Jo offered his hand and no offence was meant or taken. For some reason, I've always forgotten to ask Hawkeye if he's got that foul somewhere on film.

What he did get on film was our 'exclusive' of Richard in his Wizard kit. Bizarrely, no other photographer had bothered to ask for the picture. Goughie was coming to a strange land right enough.

We finished off with a chat with both the Scots, although I sensed Mo-Jo was happy to stay out the headlines. But he seemed happy with the new life he'd created for himself and I wished him well.

Our final question was asking him to recommend a bar for us to spend our last night in Kansas. We'd done the job we'd came to do and it was time for a bit of celebration.

He recommended a club somewhere in the city centre and promised us we'd have a good time there. After a shower and a bite back at our hotel, we jumped in a cab to try it out.

The club was up a back street – like all good clubs should be – and had a couple of bouncers on the door. We paid $10 admission and walked up stairs and through a curtain.

In was almost pitch black inside, except for a stage with a single spotlight and shiney, silver pole. Clinging to it was a blonde girl who appeared to have forgotten to put on her clothes!

This wasn't what we had in mind, but after shelling out ten bucks each, we thought we'd stay for a little while.

A topless waitress came over to our table for an order. Hawkeye and I tried to act cool – as if topless girls are standard in Glasgow's boozers. But we were still in a state of shock.

'Two beers please,' said Hawkeye.

'Sorry, sir, but we don't have any beer.'

'Do you have Bacardi?'

'No, sir, we have no liquor at all. We have an entertainments licence – but no liquor licence.'

No swally? What kind of f*****g club was this?

'Next time we see that Mo-Jo, I'll f*****g kick him,' said Hawkeye.

We decided that watching naked girls was all very well … but not with a soda pop. It was time to go.

On the way out, we passed the bouncers we'd met barely five minutes before on the way in.

'Not your kind of place, guys?' one of them sneered.

The inference was clear – they thought we were a couple of gays who had strayed into the wrong club. Hawkeye was incensed.

But I grabbed his arm and told him it wasn't worth it. We found a pub with live music and local-brew beers just around the corner.

And it sold the kind of steaks Hoss Cartwright from *Bonanza* would have been proud of.